The World's Easiest Guide

to

Using the APA

Carol J. Amato

STARGAZER
Publishing Company
Westminster, California

Published by Stargazer Publishing Company
PO Box 2178
Westminster, CA 92683
(800) 606-7895
(714) 531-6342
FAX (714) 531-8898

Edited by Claudia Suzanne

All material in this book corresponds to the Fourth Edition of the *Publication Manual of the American Psychological Association*. This book is intended for undergraduate use; therefore, elements that pertain to the typesetting requirements of the *APA Journal* have been omitted.

ISBN: 0-9643853-4-1 (College Edition, spiral bound)
        0-9643853-5-X (Library Edition, perfect bound)

Library of Congress Catalog Card Number: 94-92420

Dedication

To all of the students at the
University of Phoenix

Table of Contents

Chapter 5 Documenting Your Sources in the Text, Cont'd.

Chapter 6 Formatting the Frontis Material and Appendices 91

Chapter 7 Creating a Bibliography or List of References 113

Chapter 7 Creating a Bibliography or List of References, *Cont'd.*

Chapter 7 *Creating a Bibliography or List of References*, *Cont'd.*

List of Figures

List of Tables

Introduction

The World's Easiest Guide to Using the APA gives under-graduate and graduate students a simple, clearcut explanation of how to use the American Psychological Association (APA) style guide in formatting their reports and research projects. It is also designed as a guide for faculty who are teaching students this particular style.

What is a style guide?

All departments in colleges and universities require that students' papers be presented in the same manner. They each have a specific way sources must be documented in the bibliography or list of references. The books that supply these directions are called style guides. A style guide not only shows how to document sources, however, but also explains the rules for creating many other parts of the document, such as:

- which font (typestyle) to use

- how to create and place headers and footers

- the number of lines per page (i.e., whether you should single- or double-space the document)

- whether to use upper- or lower-case on certain words, titles, names, etc.

- how to space out such items as mathematical symbols or equations and scientific formulas

- how to document paraphrased material and direct quotations from other sources

- whether the document should be printed single-sided or double-sided

- how to place figures and tables

There are many style guides. Among the ones commonly used in colleges and universities are:

- MLA (Modern Language Association)

- Chicago (The University of Chicago Manual of Style)

- APA

All psychology and nursing departments, most education departments, and most business schools use the APA.

If you are a business, nursing, or education, rather than psychology, student, you may not be familiar with the APA style, and may be wondering why you must use it. For some unknown reason, these disciplines have chosen to use the APA style as the standard for their theses, projects, and dissertations.

If you took an introductory psychology course, you might have been introduced to the APA through such sources as *Form and Style* (Appendix B), *A Writer's Reference*, or either the gray or burgundy style guide put out by the APA itself.

Why aren't these sources enough?

Appendix B of *Form and Style* shows only how to do a list of references using the APA. It does not explain how to set up the pages of a report or project or how to document sources within the body. *A Writer's Reference* contains only a few pages of explanation. The *APA Style Guide* does explain everything, but is really geared for professional psychologists submitting articles to the American Psychological Association's own journal; therefore, some of the guidelines are very confusing and/or do not apply to formatting reports or projects at the undergraduate level. Writing a report or project is formidable enough without having to tackle the complexities of the APA's *Publication Manual*.

I hope that *The World's Easiest Guide to Using the APA* proves to be just that for you.

Chapter 1
Setting Up Your Pages

A report or project includes the following:

- Title page

- Executive Summary (optional)

- Table of Contents

- List of Figures (if more than three)

- List of Tables (if more than three)

- Dedication (optional, and only for theses, projects, and dissertations)

- Body of document

- References

- Appendix(ces) (optional for a report)

This chapter talks about creating the body pages of a document. It includes specific instructions on the following:

- Using the correct font

- Elements of a project page

    √ Setting the margins
    √ Formatting the header
    √ Formatting the headings
    √ Creating body text
    √ Formatting the page numbers

Using the Correct Font

With the availability of desktop-publishing programs today, it's easy to feel that one should create fancy covers and use various fonts to make a document look good. As nice as this might appear, you must use *manuscript* style; that is, doublespacing with roughly 25 lines per page. That means just plain type, folks, just plain type.

Use one of the following fonts in 12-point size:

- Courier

- Courier New

- Times

- Times Roman

- Times New Roman

Figure 1 shows examples of these fonts.

If you are using Microsoft Word 2.0 for Windows or WordPerfect 6.0 for Windows, you may encounter the following:

- *Microsoft Word 2.0*

  Times Roman seems to have a hard time conforming to the margins. When the page is printed, it runs past the right-hand margin. In addition, wherever a word is italicized, it prints over itself, and the result is a very messy page. Test a page out before using this font.

- *WordPerfect 5.2/6.0 for Windows*

  WordPerfect borrows the Courier font names from their old typewriter counterparts. Courier 12 is Elite typesize and Courier 10 is Pica typesize; therefore, Courier 10 is bigger than Courier 12. This is exactly the opposite of other word processors, including Word 2.0, which determine font size by "point" size (i.e., the height of the letter).

```
This is Courier

This is Courier New
```

This is Times

This is Times Roman

This is Times New Roman

Figure 1. Examples of Acceptable Fonts.

Elements of a Document Page

Your document's pages will consist of the following elements:

- Margins

- Header

- Headings

- Body text

- Graphics

This section explains how to create the margins, header, headings, and body text. Detailed information on how to place graphics is explained in Chapter 2.

Setting the Margins

Set the margins of your document to the following:

- Left margin = 1"

- Top margin = 1"

- Right margin = 1"

- Bottom margin = 1"

Refer to Figure 2.

EXCEPTION: If you intend to bind your document, you may set the left margin to 1½".

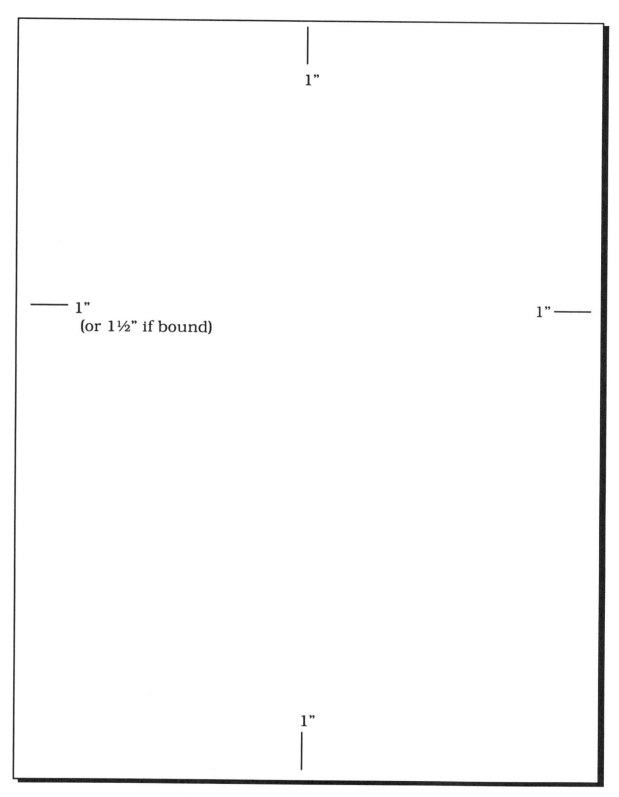

Figure 2. Correct Margin Settings.

Formatting the Header

Each of your pages must have a header consisting of the following:

- Short version of the title (50 characters maximum)

- Page number

Let's say that the full title of your report or project is "Problems with Reorganization Factors at ABC Company." The short title can be "Reorganization Factors."

The short title and the page number are on the same line; leave five spaces between the two, as shown in Figure 3. This format is called a "page header"; it must appear on every page of your document. Check the documentation provided with your word-processing program for instructions on how to set up the header.

Appendices A through E show examples of full reports and chapters with a page header.

Reorganization Factors   23

Lorem ipsum dolor sit amet, consectetuer adipisci elit, sed diam nonummy nibh eusmod tin cidunt ut loreet dolore magna aliquam erat volutpat. Ut wisi ad minim veniam, quis nostrud exerci tation ulcorper suscipit lobortis nisl ut aliquip ex ea commodo consequat.

Duis atem vel eum iriure dolor in hendrerit in putate velit esse molestie consequat, vel illum dolore feugiat nulla facilisis at vero eros et accumsan et odio dignissim qui blandit praesent luptatum zzril del augue duis dolore te feugait nulla facilisi.

Nam liber tempor cum soluta nobis eleifend id congue nihil imperdiet doming id quod mazim placerat possim assum.

Lorem ipsum dolor sit amet, consectetuer adipisci elit, sed diam nonummy nibh euismod tin cidunt ut loreet odio dignissim qui blandit praesent luptatum zzril del dolore magna aliquam erat volutpat. Ut wisi enim minim veniam, quis nostrud exerci tation ullamcorper.

Figure 3. Example Header.

Formatting the Headings

Determining the Number of Levels

Headings (as opposed to head-*ers*) are the section titles in your document. For instance, a report might have the following headings:

- Introduction

- Body Headings (example: "Findings")

- Conclusion and Recommendations

This setup uses one heading level; however, if the body were further subdivided into subheadings, two heading levels would exist (i.e., dividing "Findings" into "Attitudes Among Management Personnel" and "Attitudes Among Employees").

Every heading level must contain at least two listings; otherwise, incorporate the material into the heading above that level. In other words, you cannot have just one subheading under "Findings"; you must have at least two.

Figure 4 shows an example of the headings for Chapter 1 of a University of Phoenix (UOP) Business Research Project. As you can see, this chapter uses three levels of headings. That is, it divides the information into three levels of importance:

- The title of the chapter   (1st level heading)

- The main heading level   (2nd level heading)

- One subheading level   (3rd level heading)

Let's say you are using the format shown in Figure 4. You may decide to further subdivide the heading "Dependent and Independent Variables" into "Dependent Variables" and "Independent Variables." If so, you have now reached four levels of headings (see page 20.) Some of the sections of other chapters may include a fifth level heading (see page 22).

```
                Chapter 1   (Level 1)
                Introduction (Level 1)

     The Research Problem   (Level 2)
        Problem Statement/Purpose (Level 3)
        Background of the Problem (Level 3)
        Research Questions (Level 3)

     Operational Definitions (Level 2)
        Dependent and Independent Variables (Level 3)
        Technical and Other Terms (Level 3)

     Hypotheses and Sample (Level 2)
        Hypotheses (Level 3)
        Scope (Level 3)
        Limitations (Level 3)

     General Procedures (Level 2)

     Summary (Level 2)
```

Figure 4. Levels of Headings Used in Chapter 1 of the UOP's Business Research Project.

Selecting the Heading Styles

The APA requires you to use different heading *styles* depending on the number of heading *levels* you have. While the APA *Publication Manual* itself refers to these styles as "levels," they are called "styles" in this book to avoid confusion with the levels of importance you are using in your report or chapter. *The World's Easiest Guide* does follow the APA numbering system for these styles, however. Therefore, then, the APA has five heading styles, as shown in Figure 5. In this figure, "flush left" refers to flush with the *margin*—not with the edge of the paper.

This section shows the styles to use for the different numbers of heading levels. Most short reports use one or two heading levels; comprehensive reports, projects, and theses may use three or more.

To determine which styles to use, count the number of heading levels in your report or select the chapter of your thesis or project that contains the most heading levels and turn to the instructions in this book for that number of headings:

1 heading level	page 14
2 heading levels	page 16
3 heading levels	page 18
4 heading levels	page 20
5 heading levels	page 22

Use the selected set of headings throughout your document. Pay close attention to the upper/lower case requirements.

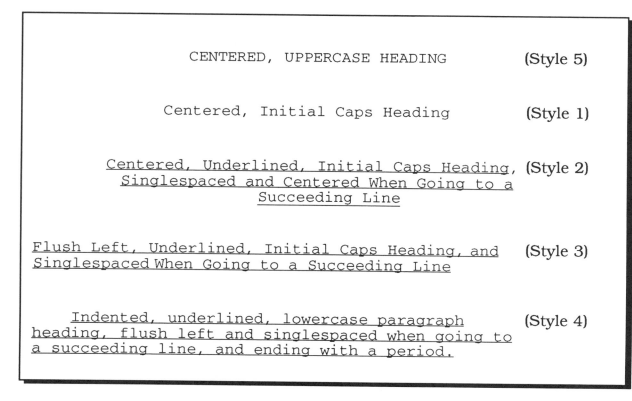

Figure 5. *The Five APA Heading Styles.*

Using One Heading Level

Table 1 shows the correct style for one heading level: APA style 1.

Table 1. Correct Style for One Heading Level.

LEVEL	APA STYLE	DESCRIPTION
1	1	Centered, With Initial Caps

Figure 6 shows an example of the heading style for one heading level. See Appendix A for a complete sample report with one heading level.

NOTE: The title of the report and the other headings are all level 1 headings.

NOTE: The title "Introduction" is not used in the APA style, because this section is identified by its position in the document.

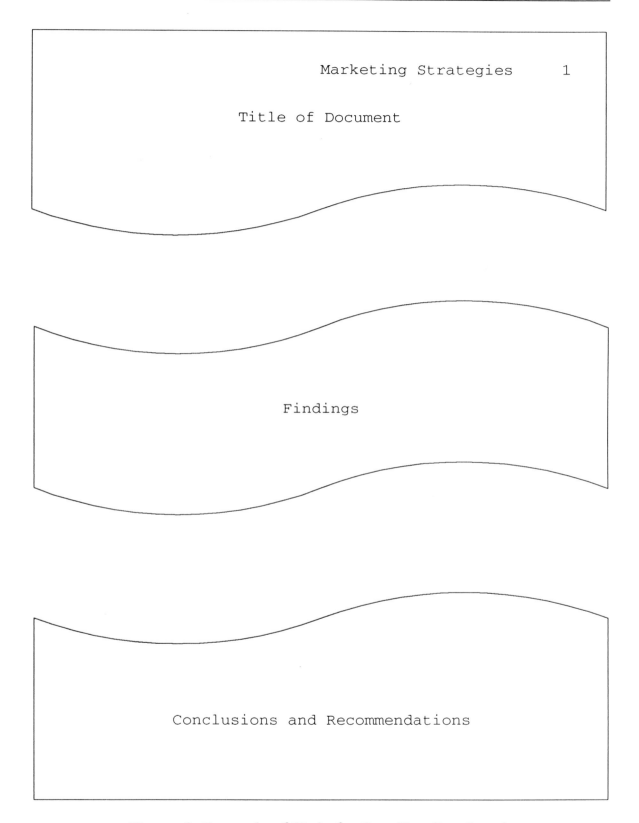

Figure 6. Example of Style for One Heading Level.

Using Two Heading Levels

Table 2 shows the correct styles for two heading levels: APA styles 1 and 3.

Table 2. Correct Styles for Two Heading Levels.

LEVEL	APA STYLE	DESCRIPTION
1	1	Centered, With Initial Caps
2	3	Flush Left, Underlined, With Initial Caps

Figure 7 shows an example of the styles to use for two heading levels. See Appendix B for a complete sample report with two heading levels.

NOTE: The title of the report is the same level as the level 1 headings; therefore, it also uses style 1.

NOTE: The title "Introduction" is not used in the APA style, because this section is identified by its position in the document.

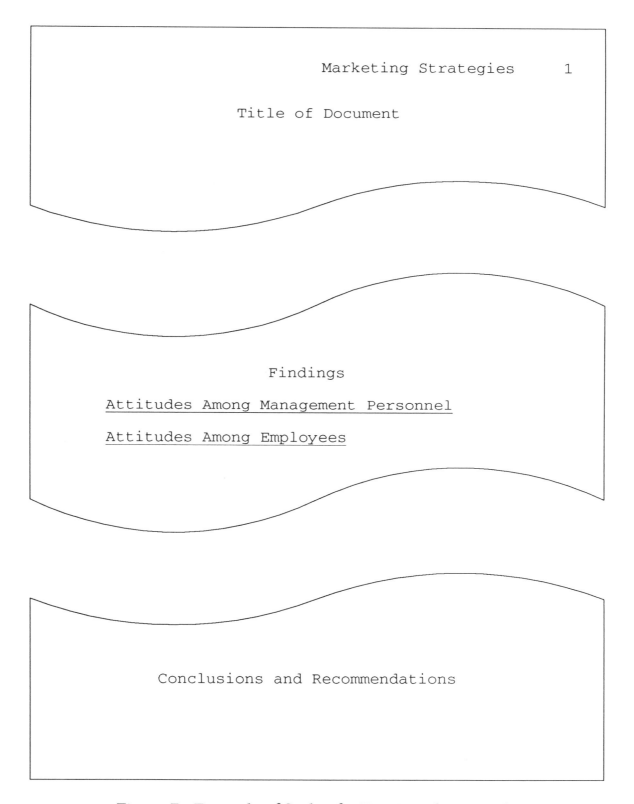

Figure 7. Example of Styles for Two Heading Levels.

Using Three Heading Levels

Table 3 shows the correct styles for three heading levels: APA styles 1, 3, and 4:

Table 3. Correct Styles for Three Heading Levels.

LEVEL	APA STYLE	DESCRIPTION
1	1	Centered, With Initial Caps
2	3	Flush Left, Underlined, With Initial Caps
3	4	Indented, underlined, with lowercase words, flush left and singlespaced when going to a succeeding line, and ending with a period.

Chapter 1 of the UOP Business Research Project uses a minimum of three heading levels, so it is used as the example in Figure 8. Note the underlined period at the end of the level 4 heading and the lowercase words.

See Appendix C for a complete sample with three heading levels.

NOTE: Unlike the title of a report (see pages 14 and 16), the title of a chapter is a level 1 heading by itself; the first headings in the chapter text descend to level 2 headings.

NOTE: The title "Introduction" is not used in the APA style, because this section is identified by its position in the document.

In the example in Figure 8, however, the word "Introduction" is included because it is part of the chapter title.

If you are writing a report or article, put the report or article title where the chapter title is in Figure 8.

Chapter 1

Introduction

The Research Problem

    Problem statement/purpose.

    Background of the problem.

    Research questions.

Operational Definitions

    Dependent and independent variables.

    Technical and other terms.

Hypotheses and Sample

    Hypotheses.

    Scope.

    Limitations.

General Procedures

Summary

Figure 8. Example of Styles for Three Heading Levels.

Using Four Heading Levels

Table 4 shows the correct styles for four heading levels: APA styles 1, 2, 3, and 4.

Table 4. Correct Styles for Four Heading Levels.

LEVEL	APA STYLE	DESCRIPTION
1	1	Centered, With Initial Caps
2	2	Centered, Underlined, With Initial Caps
3	3	Flush Left, Underlined, With Initial Caps
4	4	Indented, underlined, with lowercase words, flush left and singlespaced when going to a succeeding line, and ending with a period.

Figure 9 shows another example of Chapter 1 of the UOP Business Research Project, this time using four heading levels. This example is four levels because the Dependent and Independent Variables heading has been divided further into two subheadings: Dependent Variables and Independent Variables. Note the underlined period at the end of the level 4 heading.

See Appendix D for a complete sample chapter with four heading levels.

NOTE: Unlike the title of a report (see pages 14 and 16), the title of a chapter is a level one heading by itself; the first headings in the chapter text descend to level 2 headings.

NOTE: The title "Introduction" is not used in the APA style, because this section is identified by its position in the document.

In the example in Figure 9, however, the word "Introduction" is included because it is part of the chapter title.

If you are writing a report or article, put the report or article title where the chapter title is in Figure 9.

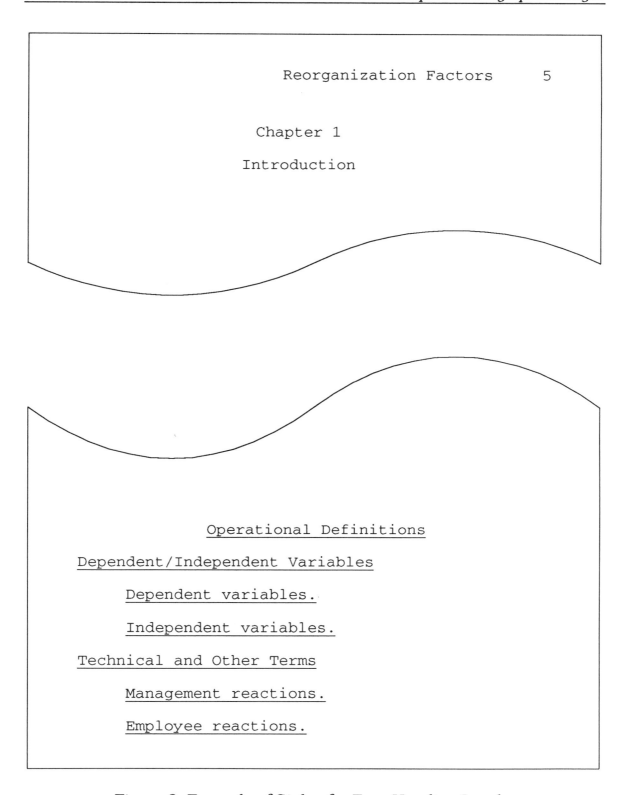

Figure 9. Example of Styles for Four Heading Levels.

Using Five Heading Levels

Table 5 shows the correct styles for five heading levels: APA styles 5, 1, 2, 3, and 4.

Table 5. Correct Styles for Five Heading Levels.

LEVEL	APA STYLE	DESCRIPTION
1	5	CENTERED, UPPERCASE
2	1	Centered, With Initial Caps
3	2	<u>Centered, Underlined, With Initial Caps</u>
4	3	<u>Flush Left, Underlined, With Initial Caps</u>
5	4	<u>Indented, underlined, with lowercase words, flush left and singlespaced when going to a succeeding line, and ending with a period.</u>

Figure 10 shows an example of five heading levels for Chapter 4 of the UOP Business Research Project. See Appendix E for a complete sample chapter with five heading levels. Note the underlined period at the end of the level 5 heading.

NOTE: Unlike the title of a report (see pages 14 and 16), the title of a chapter is a level one heading by itself; the first headings in the chapter text descend to level 2 headings.

NOTE: The title "Introduction" is not used in the APA style, because this section is identified by its position in the document.

In the example in Figure 10, however, the word "Introduction" is included because it is part of the chapter title.

If you are writing a report or article, put the report or article title where the chapter title is Figure 10.

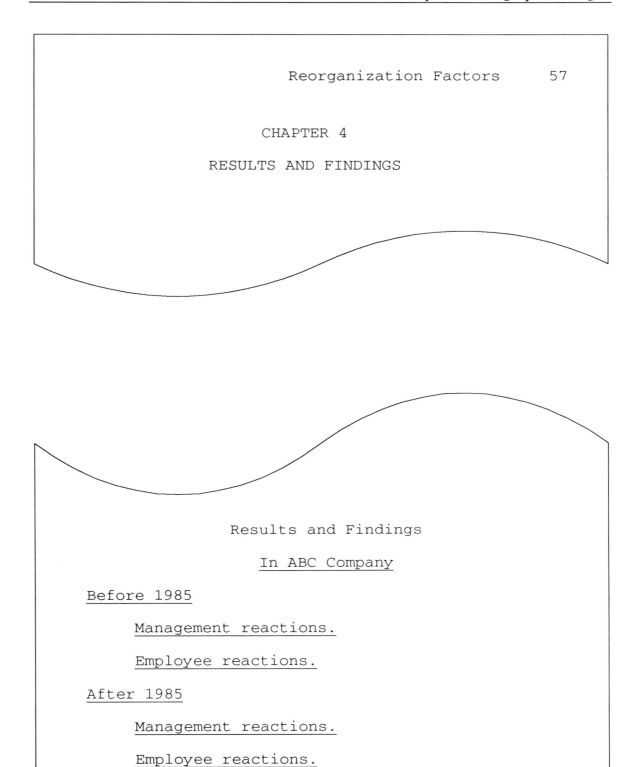

Figure 10. Example of Styles for Five Heading Levels.

Creating Body Text

Follow these rules when creating the body text:

1. Type your text double-spaced, printed on *one* side of the page.

CAUTION!

If you photocopy your document, do *not* create a double-sided version!

---

2. Type approximately 25 lines per page. See Appendices A through E for sample pages.

3. Use a *ragged-right* margin for your pages. A ragged right margin has lines of differing length, as shown in Figure 11. Compare it to the example in Figure 12, which shows a *right-justified* margin.

   A right-justified margin makes the document more difficult to read because the computer adds extra spaces between the words to make the lines end evenly. If you look closely at the text in Figure 12, you can see those extra spaces. Ragged-right margins are kinder to your instructor.

4. Indent the first line of each paragraph five spaces.

5. Doublespace between paragraphs—do not quad-ruplespace!

CAUTION!

Strict APA guidelines require no hyphenation in document text. This rule is meant to prevent problems when typesetting a document for the *APA Journal*. Since undergraduate papers will not be typeset, some of the examples in this book show hyphenation. Check your school's or department's requirements before hyphenating any of your text.

Duis atem vel eum iriure dolor in hendrerit in vulputate velit esse molestie consequat, vel illum dolore eu feugiat nulla facilisis at vero eros et accumsan et iusto odio dignissim qui blandit praesent luptatum zzril delenit augue duis dolore te feugait nulla facilisi.

Figure 11. Example of Text With Ragged Right Margin.

Duis atem vel eum iriure dolor in hendrerit in vulputate velit esse molestie consequat, vel illum dolore eu feugiat nulla facilisis at vero eros et accumsan et iusto odio dignissim qui blandit praesent luptatum zzril delenit augue duis dolore te feugait nulla facilisi.

Figure 12. Example of Text With Justified Right Margin.

Formatting the Page Numbers

Number your document with Arabic numerals starting from the title page. Place the page number about five spaces from the header. Figure 13 shows a sample of a first page of a report with the page number in the correct position. Figure 14 shows a sample of the first page of Chapter 1 of a UOP business research project with the page number in the correct position.

NOTE: Figure 14 shows the word "Introduction" because it is part of the chapter title (see page 14).

Reorganization Factors   5

Problems With Reorganization Factors

at ABC Company

Lorem ipsum dolor sit amet, consectetuer adipisci elit, sed diam nonummy nibh eusmod tin cidunt ut loreet dolore magna aliquam erat volutpat. Ut wisi ad minim veniam, quis nostrud exerci tation ulcorper suscipit lobortis nisl ut aliquip ex ea commodo consequat.

Duis atem vel eum iriure dolor in hendrerit in putate velit esse molestie consequat, vel illum dolore feugiat nulla facilisis at vero eros et accumsan et odio dignissim qui blandit praesent luptatum zzril del augue duis dolore te feugait nulla facilisi.

Nam liber tempor cum soluta nobis eleifend id congue nihil imperdiet doming id quod mazim placerat possim assum.

Lorem ipsum dolor sit amet, consectetuer adipisci elit, sed diam nonummy nibh euismod tin cidunt ut loreet dolore magna aliquam erat volutpat. Ut wisi enim minim veniam, quis nostrud exerci tation ullamcorper.

Figure 13. Example of First Page of a Report Showing Page Numbering.

Reorganization Factors   5

Chapter 1

Introduction

Lorem ipsum dolor sit amet, consectetuer adipisci elit, sed diam nonummy nibh eusmod tin cidunt ut loreet dolore magna aliquam erat volutpat. Ut wisi ad minim veniam, quis nostrud exerci tation ulcorper suscipit lobortis nisl ut aliquip ex ea commodo consequat.

Duis atem vel eum iriure dolor in hendrerit in putate velit esse molestie consequat, vel illum dolore feugiat nulla facilisis at vero eros et accumsan et odio dignissim qui blandit praesent luptatum zzril del augue duis dolore te feugait nulla facilisi.

Nam liber tempor cum soluta nobis eleifend id congue nihil imperdiet doming id quod mazim placerat possim assum.

Lorem ipsum dolor sit amet, consectetuer adipisci elit, sed diam nonummy nibh euismod tin cidunt ut loreet dolore magna aliquam erat volutpat. Ut wisi enim minim congue nihil imperdiet doming id quod mazim placerat veniam, quis nostrud exerci tation ullamcorper.

Figure 14. Example of First Page of a Project Chapter 1 Showing Page Numbering.

Chapter 2

Placing Graphics

Graphics are very important in your document. The saying, "A picture is worth a thousand words," is very true. Graphics help your readers understand information that is difficult to get across in words.

Your document can include two types of graphics:

- Figures

- Tables

This chapter explains how to place each of these on the page.

Placing Figures

Figures include diagrams, pictures, photos, line drawings, bar and line graphs, pie charts, etc. If you include a figure, refer to it by number in your text:

Figure 1 shows the Model 300 ergonomic desk.

or

The Model 300 ergonomic desk is available in

three styles (see Figure 1).

Then place the figure as closely as possible to that reference; that means on the same or very next page. While your figure can be narrower than the required margins of the page, it cannot be wider.

Each figure must have a sequential number and a caption. The caption need not be a complete sentence, but it should accurately describe the contents of the artwork. Place the caption below the artwork, as shown in Figure 15.

Number figures separately from tables; i.e., Figure 1, Figure 2, Figure 3, and Table 1, Table 2, Table 3—*not* Figure 1, Table 2, Figure 3. (For information on table placement, see *Placing Tables*, page 32.)

Notice that the word "Figure" and the figure number are underlined, but that the caption itself is in plain type. A period follows the figure number. Note that the figure caption immediately follows the figure number and that when the caption goes onto a second line, it is doublespaced.

Label each of the axes, placing the label parallel to its axis. Keep the labels short; use no more than two words or 10 characters. Use tick marks on both axes. Number and letter the grid points horizontally as shown in Figure 15. Be sure to include a legend.

Ergonomic Needs of ABC Company   57

Lorem ipsum dolor sit amet, consectetuer adipiscing,
sed nonummy nibh euismod tin cidunt ut laoreet dolore magna
aliquam volutpat. Ut wisi enim ad minim veniam, quis
nostrud exerci tation ullam corper suscipit lobortis nisl ut
aliquip ex ea commodo.

Duis atem vel eum iriure dolor in hendrerit in vulpu
tate velit esse molestie consequat, vel illum dolore eu
feugiat nulla facilisi. Lorem ipsum dolor sit amet, aliquip
as shown in Figure 5:

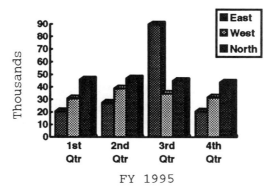

Figure 5. Nam liber tempor cum soluta nobis eleifend option
congue nihil imperdiet doming id quod mazim placerat facer
possim assum.

Figure 15. Example of Figure and Figure Caption Placement.

Placing Tables

Tables compare large amounts of data in columns. A table can be used to compare results in certain categories for test groups, for instance. If you include a table, refer to it by number in your text:

> Table 4 shows the comparisons for the 10
>
> test groups.

or

> The comparisons for the 10 test groups
>
> vary substantially (see Table 4).

Then place the table as closely as possible to that reference; i.e., that means on the same page or the very next page. While your table can be narrower than the required margins of the page, it cannot be wider.

Each table must have a sequential number and a caption. The caption need not be a complete sentence, but it should accurately describe the contents of the table.

Number tables separately from the figures; i.e., Table 1, Table 2, Table 3, and Figure 1, Figure 2, Figure 3—*not* Table 1, Figure 2, Table 3. (For information on figure placement, see *Placing Figures*, page 30.) Place the caption at the top of the table, as shown in Figure 16.

Notice that the word "Table" and the number are in plain type, and that the caption itself is on the line *below* the word "Table." In addition, the caption is underlined—exactly the opposite of the format for a figure caption. Note also that when the caption goes onto a second line, it is doublespaced.

NOTE: Strict APA guidelines suggest using spacing rather than vertical rules in tables due to typesetting requirements for the *APA Journal.* Since undergraduate papers will not be typeset for the *Journal,* it's pointless not to use the automatic table and line generators in current word processing programs. Check your school's requirements first, however.

Ergonomic Needs of ABC Company   57

Lorem ipsum dolor sit amet, consectetuer adipiscing, sed nonummy nibh euismod tin cidunt ut laoreet dolore magna aliquam volutpat. Ut wisi enim ad minim veniam, quis nostrud exerci tation ullam corper.

Duis atem vel eum iriure dolor in hendrerit in vulpu tate velit esse molestie consequat, vel illum dolore eu consecatus as shown in Table 3:

Table 3

Nam liber tempor cum soluta nobis eleifend option congue nihil imperdiet doming id quod mazim placerat facer possim.

COMPANY	FEATURES						
	Adj. Hght.	Kybd Tray	Book-shelf	Cup-brd.	Draw-ers	Chair incl.	Diff. Colors
ABC	X	X	X	X	X		X
XYZ		X		X	X	X	
ACME	X	X			X		
ACE		X	X		X		X

Nam liber tempor cum soluta nobis eleifend id congue nihil imperdiet doming id quod mazim placerat possim assum. Sed nonummy nibh euismod tin cidunt ut laoreet dolore magna

Figure 16. Example of Table and Table Caption Placement.

Chapter 3

Formatting Mathematical and Statistical Material

If you are writing a comprehensive report, you may need to include other kinds of information, such as:

- mathematical symbols or equations

- statistical material

If you are writing a thesis or project, you will definitely include mathematical and statistical material. This chapter explains how to format your statistics per the APA style guide. It assumes that you already understand and have performed statistical analyses.

Formatting Mathematical Material

Citing statistical and mathematical references is easiest when using a computer. Most modern word processors have a Symbol font that allows you to place any statistical or mathematical symbol on the page. Creating some of these symbols on a typewriter is impossible, which means you must draw them by hand.

This section shows you how to format:

- equations

- displayed equations in the text

- superscripted characters

- subscripted characters

Formatting an Equation

When you type short and simple mathematical copy, space it out just the way you would a sentence with words, as shown in Figure 17. Place it all on one line, using brackets and parentheses to make the related parts of the equation clear to the reader.

Notice that there are no spaces between brackets and parentheses, or between parentheses and the first number, but there are spaces between the other elements of the equation. Study this example closely for spacing requirements.

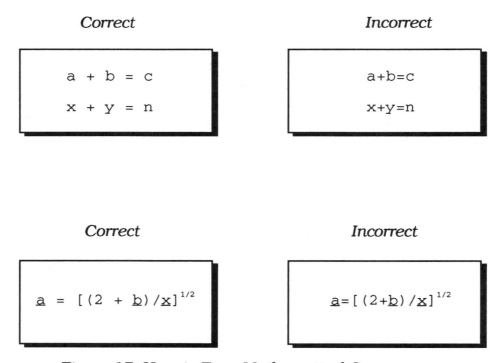

Figure 17. How to Type Mathematical Copy.

Formatting a Displayed Equation in the Text

When an equation takes up more than one line of space, you must place it by itself, just as you would a figure or table. Skip two lines before and after the equation. Figure 18 shows an example.

Number displayed equations consecutively, and place the number in parentheses at the right margin. When referring to the equation in the text, refer to it as "Equation *n*" (i.e., the word "Equation" and then its number). For example, the equation in Figure 18 would be referred to as Equation 1.

Lorem ipsum dolor sit amet, consectateur adipiscing

elit, sed diam nonummy nibh euismod tin cidunt ut laoreet

dolore magna aliquam erat voluptat:

$$\underline{b} = \sqrt{\frac{2 + \underline{b}}{\underline{x}}} \tag{1}$$

Duis atem vel eum iriure dolor in hendrerit in vulpu-

tate vlit esse molestie consequat, vel illum dolore eu feugiat

nulla facilisis at vero eros et accumsan et iusto.

Figure 18. Placement of a Displayed Equation in the Text.

Formatting a Superscripted Character

A "superscripted" character is raised above the normal line of the text. Figure 19 shows Einstein's famous equation, which has a superscripted "2" on the MC. Most word processors have a superscript command to allow automatic placement of these characters.

Correct   *Incorrect*

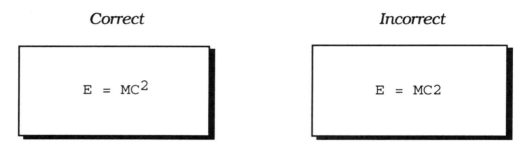

$$E = MC^2$$

$$E = MC2$$

Figure 19. Correct Format for a Superscripted Character.

Formatting a Subscripted Character

A "subscripted" character is dropped below the normal line of the text. Figure 20 shows the chemical composition of water; it has a subscripted "2" between the "H" and "O." Most word processors have a superscript command to allow automatic placement of these characters.

Correct   *Incorrect*

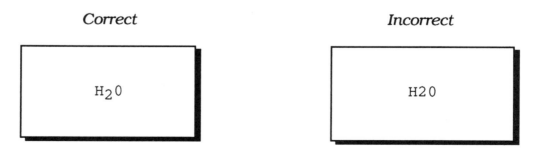

$$H_2O$$

$$H2O$$

Figure 20. Correct Format for a Subscripted Character.

Formatting Statistical Material

When formatting statistical material, follow these few simple rules:

1. If the statistic is common one, you need not include the reference for it. Include the reference only if the statistic is new or used in a controversial way.

2. If the formula for the statistic is a common one, do not include it in your text. Give formulas only for statistics that are new or rare, or extremely essential to your document.

This section shows you how to format:

- Inferential statistics

- Observed statistics

- Sample statistics

- Subject statistics

Formatting Inferential Statistics

There are three types of inferential statistics:

- *t* tests

- *F* tests

- chi-square tests

When you format any of these types of statistics, be sure to include enough information so the reader can corroborate your analyses.

Formatting *t* test Statistics

Format t test statistics as shown in Figure 21. Notice that the "t" is underlined and is lowercase. Place spaces only before and after the equal sign.

$$\underline{t}(50) = 1.5$$

Figure 21. Example of the Formatting for a t test Statistic.

Formatting *F* test Statistics

Format F test statistics as shown in Figure 22. In this example, there are two F test statistics; hence, "Fs" rather than "F." Notice that the "F" is underlined and is uppercase. Pay close attention to the spacing.

$$\underline{F}s(3, 125) = 4.25 \text{ and } 3.95$$

Figure 22. Example of the Formatting for an F test Statistic.

Formatting Chi-Square Statistics

Format chi-square test statistics as shown in Figure 23. Place the degrees of freedom and sample size in parentheses. Notice that the "N" is uppercase and the "p" is lowercase and that both are underlined. Pay close attention to the spacing.

$$\chi^2(6, \underline{N} = 300) = 8.57, \underline{p} < .05$$

Figure 23. Example of the Formatting for a Chi-Square Statistic.

Formatting Observed Statistics

Observed statistics, which may be sample statistics, are shown by using lowercase Greek letters. Figure 24 shows an example. The "χ^2" represents the observed-type sample statistic.

$$\chi^2(6, \underline{N} = 300) = 8.57, \underline{p} < .05$$

Figure 24. Example of the Formatting for Observed Statistics.

Formatting Sample Statistics

Sample statistics are expressed by using Latin letters, such as "*SD*" for Standard Deviation. An example is shown in Figure 25.

$$\underline{SD} = 5.45$$

Figure 25. Example of the Formatting for Sample Statistics.

Formatting Subject Statistics

Point out the number of subjects in a total sample by using an uppercase, underlined "N." Use a lowercase, underlined "n" to represent the number of subjects in a portion of the total sample. Figure 26 shows some examples. The number "350" represents the total sample; therefore, the capital "N" is used. The number "25" represents a portion of that sample; therefore, the lowercase "n" is used.

$$\underline{N} = 350$$

$$\underline{n} = 25$$

Figure 26. Examples of the Formatting for Subject Statistics.

Formatting Statistical Symbols

Refer to Table 6 if you are not sure how to format a particular statistical symbol.

Table 6. Statistical Abbreviations and Symbols.

SYMBOL	DEFINITION	SYMBOL	DEFINITION
A_2	Control chart factor for means	μ	Population mean
a	Y-intercept	Q_1	First quartile
A.D.	Average deviation	Q_3	Third quartile
ANOVA	Analysis of variance	Q	Quantity index
b	Slope of the regression line	Q.D.	Quartile deviation
c	Mean number of defects per unit	r^2	Coefficient of deviation
χ^2	Chi-square statistic	r_s	Rank-order correlation coefficient
$_nC_r$	Combination of *n* things taken at *r* time	r	Sample correlation coefficient
C.V.	Coefficient of variation	ρ	Population coefficient of correlation
CPI	Consumer Price Index	σ^2	Population variance
D_4	Control limit factor for the range	σ_p	Standard error of the proportion
EMV	Expected monetary value	σ	Population standard deviation
EQL	Expected opportunity loss	σ_2	Standard error of the mean
EVPI	Expected value of perfect information	s_d	Standard deviation of paired differences
f_e	Expected frequency	s^2	Sample variance
f_o	Observed frequency	$s_{y'x}$	Standard error of estimate
F	*F*-distribution	s	Sample standard deviation
G.M.	Geometric mean	sk	Coefficient of skewness
H	Kruskal-Wallis test statistic	SD	Standard deviation
H_0	Null hypothesis under test	SS total	Sum of squares total
H_1	Alternative hypothesis	SSB	Sum of squares blocks
k	Number of independent variables	SSE	Sum of squares error
MSE	Mean square error	SSR	Sum of squares regression
MSTR	Mean square treatment	SST	Sum of squares treatments
n	Number of items in the sample	T^2	Treatment column total
N	Number of items in the population	t	Student's *t*-distribution

Table 6. Statistical Abbreviations and Symbols, Cont'd.

SYMBOL	DEFINITION	SYMBOL	DEFINITION
$_nP_r$	Permutation of *n* things taken *r* at a time	U	Mann-Whitney U statistic
ρ_c	Weighted mean of sample proportions	V	Value index
ρ	Proportion of success in a sample	X_o	Control limit for sample mean
P	Population proportion	X_w	Weighted mean
P	Price index	X	Sample mean
P(A)	Probability of an event happening	Y	Predicted value of Y
P(A/B)	Probability of an event given that another event has happened	Z	Standard normal deviate

Chapter 4

Using Seriation and Abbreviations

Using Seriation

No doubt you will have paragraphs in your text in which you wish to state a number of points, such as a list or a set of steps, or other text that is in *series* form; hence, the word *seriation*. You can create these in two forms:

- As a list in a sentence

- As a series of steps

- As a list of points

Creating a List in a Sentence

Here's how you create a list or series of steps in a sentence. Figure 27 shows how your sentence should look.

Note that lower case letters in parentheses are used and that commas, not semi-colons, appear after each point.

```
Duis atem vel eum iriure dolor in hendrerit in vulputate
(a) velit essemolestie consequat, (b) vel illum dolore eu
feugiat nulla facilisis at vero eros et accumsan, et
(c) iusto odio dignissim qui blandit praesent luptatum
zzril delenit augue duis dolore te feugait nulla acilisi.
```

Figure 27. Example of a List in a Sentence.

Creating Steps in a Procedure

To create steps in a procedure, format your text as shown in Figure 28. Note that each step begins at the margin and that you must quadruplespace between each step.

```
Duis atem vel eum iriure dolor in hendrerit:


1. Vulputate velit esse molestie consequat, vel illum

dolore eu feugiat nulla facilisis at vero eros et

accumsan et iusto.


2. Odio dignissim qui blandit praesent luptatum zzril

delenit augue duis dolore te feugait nulla facilis.


3. Nam liber tempor cum soluta nobis eleifend option

congue nihil imperdiet doming id quod mazim placerat

facer possim assum.


4. Lorem ipsum dolor sit amet, consectetuer adipiscing

elit, sed diam nonummy nibh euismod tin cidunt ut

laoreet dolore magna aliquam erat volutpat.
```

Figure 28.   Example of Steps in a Procedure.

Creating a List of Points

To create a list of points, such as a list of conclusions or recommendations, format your text as shown in Figure 29. This format is exactly the same as that for steps in a procedure (see page 47). Each step begins at the margin and you must quadruplespace between each step.

```
Duis atem vel eum iriure dolor in hendrerit:


1. Vulputate velit esse molestie consequat, vel

illum dolore eu feugiat nulla facilisis at vero eros et

accumsan et iusto.


2. Dio dignissim qui blandit praesent luptatum zzril

delenit augue duis dolore te feugait nulla facilis.


3. Nam liber tempor cum soluta nobis eleifend option

congue nihil imperdiet doming id quod mazim placerat

facer possim assum.


4. Lorem ipsum dolor sit amet, consectetuer adipiscing

elit, sed diam nonummy nibh euismod tin cidunt ut laoreet

dolore magna aliquam erat volutpat.
```

Figure 29. Example of a List of Points.

Using Abbreviations

There are two types of abbreviations:

- Latin abbreviations

- Scientific abbreviations

The only rules to remember are:

1. Never start a sentence with a lowercase abbreviation or a symbol that stands alone.

2. Instead, capitalize the abbreviation or acronym, and capitalize the first letter of a word attached to a symbol.

Using Latin Abbreviations

Use the Latin abbreviations shown in Table 7 in parenthetical material only. Be sure to include the periods and commas as shown in this table and to avoid spaces between the elements of the abbreviation.

Use the full English meaning when referring to these items in non-parenthetical material.

As with any rule, there are exceptions. You can use the Latin abbreviations shown in Table 8 in both parenthetical and non-parenthetical material.

Table 7. Latin Abbreviations Used in Parenthetical Material and Their Meanings.

ABBREVIATION	MEANING	ABBREVIATION	MEANING
cf.	compare	i.e.,	that is
e.g.,	for example	viz.,	namely
etc.	and so forth	vs.	versus, against

Table 8. Latin Abbreviations Used in Both Parenthetical and Non-Parenthetical Material.

ABBREVIATION	MEANING	WHERE USED
v.	versus	In references and text citations of court cases
et al.	and others	In the reference list and in the text

Using Scientific Abbreviations

Scientific abbreviations that may be used with the APA style fall into four main categories:

- Units of measure

- Chemical compounds

- Medical percentage concentrations

- Medical routes of administration

Using Abbreviations for Units of Measure

Table 9 shows the abbreviations for the units of measure and their meanings. Use these abbreviations and symbols for metric and nonmetric units of measure that are accompanied by numbers (e.g., 10 cm, 25° C, 18 hr). When they are not accompanied by numbers, use the full English meaning instead.

Using Abbreviations for Chemical Compounds

Refer to chemical compounds by their common or chemical name. If you use the common name, place the chemical name in parentheses. Refrain from using chemical formulas, even if they are shorter.

If the name of an organic compound is listed as an abbreviation or acronym in the *Webster's Collegiate Dictionary* (such as "DNA" for "deoxyribonucleic acid"), you can use it without explaining its meaning.

Table 9. Abbreviations for Units of Measure.

ABBREV.	MEANING	ABBREV.	MEANING
A	ampere	mA	milliampere
Å	angstrom	mEq	milliequivalent
AC	alternating current	meV	million electron volts
a.m.	ante meridiem	mg	milligram
°C	degrees Celsius	min	minute
Ci	curie	ml	milliliter
cm	centimeter	mm	millimeter
cps	cycles per second	mM	millimolar
dB	decibel (specify scale)	mmHg	millimeters of mercury
DC	direct current	mmol	millimole
deg/s	degrees per second	mol wt	molecular weight
dl	deciliter	mph	miles per hour (convert to metric)
°F	degrees Fahrenheit	ms	millisecond
g	gram	MΩ	megohm
g	gravity	N	newton
hr	hour	ns	nanosecond
Hz	hertz	p.m.	post meridiem
in.	inch	ppm	parts per million
IQ	intelligence quotient	psi	pound per square inch (convert to metric)
IU	international unit	rpm	revolutions per minute
kg	kilogram	s	second
km	kilometer	S	siemens
kph	kilometers per hour	V	volt
kW	kilowatt	W	watt
L	Liter	μm	micrometer
m	meter		

Using Abbreviations in Concentrations

Specify solutions expressed as percentage concentrations rather than molar as a:

- Weight per volume ratio (wt/wt)

- Volume ratio (vol/vol)

- Weight ratio (wt/wt) of solution to solvent

Be sure to use a ratio for concentrations of alcohol, glucose, and sucrose.

Using Abbreviations in Routes of Administration

Abbreviate routes of administration only when they are accompanied by number-and-unit combinations. Do not use periods. Table 10 shows some examples.

Table 10. Examples of Abbreviations for Routes of Administration.

ABBREVIATION	EXPLANATION
icv	Intracerebral ventricular
im	Intramuscular
ip	Intraperitoneal
iv	Intravenous
sc	Subcutaneous

Using Abbreviations in Tables

You can use abbreviations, such as for the months of the year, in tables. Use the three-letter abbreviation, such as "Jan," "Feb," "Mar," etc. When referring to units of time in the text, however, spell them out completely, even when accompanied by a number (e.g., March 7, *not* Mar 7).

Using an Acronym

Acronyms are words formed from the initials of long terms, such as "TQM" for "Total Quality Management." Plan to use acronyms only for long, well-known terms. Then spell out the phrase completely the first time you use it. Put the acronym in parentheses, as shown in Figure 30. The next time you refer to this term, use the acronym by itself.

```
Duis atem vel eum iriure dolor in hendrerit in vulputate
velit essemolestie consequat, vel illum dolore eu feugiat
nulla facilisis at vero eros et accumsan, and is called
Total Quality Management (TQM). Dignissim qui blandit
praesent luptatum zzril delenit augue duis dolore te
feugait nulla acilisi.
```

Figure 30. Example of the First Use of an Acronym.

Formatting Plurals

To create a plural of an acronym, abbreviation, or statistical symbol, just add "s." Do not include an apostrophe. Table 11 shows some examples.

Table 11. Examples of Plurals of Abbreviations.

ABBREVIATION	EXPLANATION
IQs	Intelligence quotients
Eds.	Editors, Editions
vols.	Volumes

There are two exceptions, in which no "s" is added:

- "pp." is the correct plural for "pages"

- Units of measure do not use an "s"

Using Abbreviations in the Reference List

You can use abbreviations in the Reference list in two ways:

- For parts of books and other publications

- To indicate the state in which a publisher is located

Using Abbreviations for Parts of Books and Other Publications

You can use the abbreviations in Table 12 to indicate parts of books and other publications.

Table 12. Abbreviations to Use to Indicate Parts of Books and Other Publications in the Reference List.

ABBREVIATION	MEANING	ABBREVIATION	MEANING
chap.	chapter	p. (pp.)	page (pages)
ed.	edition	Vol.	Volume
Rev. ed.	revised edition	Vols.	Volumes
2nd ed.	second edition	No.	Number
Ed. (Eds.)	Editor (Editors)	Pt.	Part
Trans.	Translator(s)	Tech. Rep.	Technical Report
n.d.	no date	Suppl.	Supplement

Using Abbreviations to Indicate the Location of the Publisher

When referencing books in the Reference list, you must include the city where the publisher is located. If the city is not a major one, you must include the two-letter postal state code abbreviation, as shown in Table 13, or the country name.

Table 13. Two-letter Postal Code Abbreviations for States and Territories Used in Book References.

LOCATION	ABBREVIATION	LOCATION	ABBREVIATION
Alabama	AL	Missouri	MO
Alaska	AK	Montana	MT
American Samoa	AS	Nebraska	NE
Arizona	AZ	Nevada	NV
Arkansas	AR	New Hampshire	NH
California	CA	New Jersey	NJ
Canal Zone	CZ	New Mexico	NM
Colorado	CO	New York	NY
Connecticut	CT	North Carolina	NC
Delaware	DE	North Dakota	ND
District of Columbia	DC	Ohio	OH
Florida	FL	Oklahoma	OK
Georgia	GA	Oregon	OR
Guam	GU	Pennsylvania	PA
Hawaii	HI	Puerto Rico	PR
Idaho	ID	Rhode Island	RI
Illinois	IL	South Carolina	SC
Indiana	IN	South Dakota	SD
Iowa	IA	Tennessee	TN
Kansas	KS	Texas	TX
Kentucky	KY	Utah	UT
Louisiana	LA	Vermont	VT
Maine	ME	Virginia	VA
Maryland	MD	Virgin Islands	VI
Massachusetts	MA	Washington	WA
Michigan	MI	West Virginia	WV
Minnesota	MN	Wisconsin	WI
Mississippi	MS	Wyoming	WY

Chapter 5

Documenting Your Sources in the Text

During the course of writing your document, you will research many books, magazine articles, and other publications, and perhaps conduct interviews with experts in your topic. Any time you use that material in your document, you must credit the source; otherwise, you are committing plagiarism.

The APA employs a specific method for documenting sources. You must first cite the source in the text, where the borrowed material appears, then again in the list of references that follows the last page or chapter. This chapter explains how to create the in-text citations.

There are three types of in-text citations:

- *Paraphrased material*

  Perhaps you have read a book or article, or even several books or articles, and you are discussing the idea or ideas contained therein. You have not used any of the author's wording, but have explained the concepts in your own words.

- *Quotes of fewer than 40 words*

  An author's words say what you want to say, so you use those exact words. You quote fewer than 40 words from the article or book.

- *Quotes of 40 words or more*

   Here again, you use the author's words, but this time you quote 40 words or more of the book or article.

Because the ideas in paraphrased material and quotations are not your own, you must credit their sources. The APA style does *not* use footnotes. Instead, sources are credited by using what are called "parenthetical citations."

NOTE: *The citations contained in this section are not necessarily real; they have been created for example purposes.*

Citing Paraphrased Material

You can paraphrase material in two different ways:

- When you do not name the author in your sentence

- When you name the author in your sentence

Paraphrasing Material Without Naming the Author in the Sentence

With some paraphrased material, you may just state the concept; for example, perhaps you want to explain Alvin Toffler's concept of our technological future without directly quoting from his book or stating his name in the text of the sentence itself. The correct way to credit the source of this information is to type the author's last name, a comma, a space, then the year of publication, as shown in Figure 31, so the reader will know what to look up in the bibliography or reference list. Cite a magazine article the same way.

Compare these citations to those in which the author's name does appear in the text of the sentence (see page 62).

Including a Page Number

If you are paraphrasing material from a specific page or magazine article, you may even wish to include a page number, as shown in Figure 32. After the year, add a comma, a space, then a lower-case "p," a period, another space, and the page number.

Including a Range of Pages

Cite a range of pages as shown in Figure 33. Note that you must use "pp." rather than just "p."

As global conflicts fade in the East/West and North/
South, and society continues to undergo rapid
technological change, the world will experience a
deepening split between the "fast" and the "slow";
this constitutes a new division that is far more
important (Toffler, 1990).

*Figure 31. Example of an In-Text Citation of Paraphrased Material
Without Using the Author's Name in the Sentence.*

As society continues to undergo rapid technological
change, people suffer from what we now call "future
shock" (Jones, 1993, p. 24).

*Figure 32. Example of an In-Text Citation of Paraphrased Material
From a Specific Page or Magazine Article Without Using the
Author's Name in the Sentence and Showing a Page
Number.*

By the year 2000, 95% of all offices will use PCs
(Jones, 1993, pp. 24-30).

*Figure 33. Example of an In-Text Citation of Paraphrased Material
Without Using the Author's Name in the Sentence and
Covering a Range of Pages.*

Paraphrasing Material and Naming the Author in the Sentence

You may paraphrase material and include the author's name as part of your sentence, but you must still let the reader know from which publication the information came. Cite the source as shown in Figure 34.

Notice that the parenthetical citation includes just the year (and page number, if applicable) and is next to the author's name, not at the end of the sentence.

Compare these citations to those in which the author's name does not appear in the text of the sentence (see page 60).

Including a Page Number

If you are paraphrasing material from a specific page or magazine article, you may even wish to include a page number, as shown in Figure 35. After the year, add a comma, a space, then a lower-case "p," a period, another space, and the page number.

Including a Range of Pages

Cite a range of pages as shown in Figure 36. Note that you must use "pp." rather than just "p."

Toffler (1971) states that as society continues to undergo rapid technological change, people will suffer from "future shock."

Figure 34. Example of an In-Text Citation of Paraphrased Material Using the Author's Name in the Sentence.

According to Jones (1993, p. 24), as society continues to undergo rapid technological change, people will suffer from what we now call "future shock."

Figure 35. Example of an In-Text Citation of Paraphrased Material From a Specific Page or Magazine Article Using the Author's Name in the Sentence and Showing a Page Number.

Jones (1993, pp. 24-30) states that by the year 2000, 95% of all offices will use PCs.

Figure 36. Example of an In-Text Citation of Paraphrased Material Using the Author's Name in the Sentence and Covering a Range of Pages.

Citing Quotes

When you use direct quotations from people, the way you cite them depends on their length:

- Up to 40 words of manuscript text

- More than 40 words of manuscript text

Citing Up to 40 Words of Manuscript Text

Direct quotes that are up to 40 words of manuscript text are cited as part of the regular doublespaced text, as shown in Figure 37. Place the material in quotation marks to indicate that it is indeed a quote, rather than a paraphrase. Note that the citation is part of the sentence—the period is placed at the end of the entire sentence, *not* after the quotation.

He defines innovation as "the specific tool of entrepreneurs, the means by which they exploit change as an opportunity for a different business or a different service" (Drucker, 1985, p. 20), but he does not explain whether the term can be applied to reorganization and refocussing of corporations.

or

Peter Drucker (1985) defines innovation as "the specific tool of entrepreneurs, the means by which they exploit change as an opportunity for a different business or a different service" (p. 20).

Figure 37. Correct Way to Cite Up to 40 Words of Manuscript Text.

Citing 40 Words or More of Manuscript Text

When a quote takes up 40 words or more of manuscript text, indent it five spaces and doublespace it, as shown in Figure 38.

The first example in Figure 38 begins the quotation with a capital "I" because it begins a sentence. Examples 2 and 3 are continuations of the sentence begun above the quote, and so start with a lower-case letter. The page number does not appear within the parenthetical material by the author's name, but rather, in parentheses at the end of the quotation itself. In addition, the citation information at the end of the quote is outside the punctuation of the sentence.

Try to keep quotations to no more than 10 lines—there must be a way to paraphrase the material rather than lifting several pages wholesale from the original document.

```
Drucker (1985) states that:

    Innovation is the specific tool of entrepreneurs,

    the means by which they exploit change as an

    opportunity for a different business or a different

    service. Entrepreneurs need to search purposefully

    for the sources of innovation, the changes and their

    symptoms that indicate opportunities for successful

    innovation. (p. 20)
```

Figure 38. Correct Way to Cite 40 Words or More of Manuscript Text.

or

Drucker (1985) defines innovation as:

> the specific tool of entrepreneurs, the means by which they exploit change as an opportunity for a different business or a different service. Entrepreneurs need to search purposefully for the sources of innovation, the changes and their symptoms that indicate opportunities for successful innovation. (p. 20)

or

Innovation is defined as:

> the specific tool of entrepreneurs, the means by which they exploit change as an opportunity for a different business or a different service. Entrepreneurs need to search purposefully for the sources of innovation, the changes and their symptoms that indicate opportunities for successful innovation. (Drucker, 1985, p. 20)

Figure 38. Correct Way to Cite 40 Words or More of Manuscript Text, Cont'd.

Citing a Publication with Two Authors

If more than one person has written the book or article, cite it as shown in Figure 39.

When the author's names appear in the parenthetical citation, use an *ampersand* (the "&" character) instead of the word "and" between the authors' names. Use the word "and" only when the authors' names appear as part of the actual text of the sentence.

Smith and Jones (1993, p. 137) state that "by the year 2000, 95% of offices will use PCs."

or

In 1993, Smith and Jones (p. 137) stated that "by the year 2000, 95% of offices will use PCs."

or

"By the year 2000, 95% of offices will use PCs" (Smith & Jones, 1993, p. 137).

Figure 39. Examples of a Citation of a Publication With Two Authors.

Citing a Publication With Three or More Authors

Publications with three or more authors are cited according to the number of authors:

- Three, four, or five authors

- Six or more authors

If the work has three, four, or five authors, list all the authors the first time you cite the reference, put the word "and" or an ampersand between the last two authors' names (see page 68). Thereafter, cite it with the first author's name, followed by the Latin abbreviation "et al.," which means "and everyone." Figure 40 shows an example.

If the work has six or more authors, cite it as shown in Figure 40 each time.

NOTE: For subsequent citations after the first citation in a paragraph, omit the year.

```
The United States will be completely out of the reces-

sion by 1997 (Everett et al., 1993).
```

or

```
Everett et al. (1993) state that the United States will

be out of the recession by 1997.
```

Figure 40. Examples of the Subsequent Occurrence of a Citation With Three-to-Five Authors and All Citations With Six or More Authors.

EXCEPTION: If you have two similar references with the same year, cite the last names of the first authors and as many of the subsequent authors as needed to make the references

Citing Multiple Works

Cite several studies or works that all have the same common thread, philosophy, concepts, or conclusions as shown in Figure 41. List the authors in alphabetical order, using a semicolon between each of the citations.

```
Several studies (Chan & Jefferson, 1985; Gomez, 1989;

Thompson, 1992) show that....
```

Figure 41. Example of a Citation of Multiple Works.

Citing an Author with More Than One Publication in the Same Year

What if an author has more than one publication in the same year? Since the reader must be able to tell which listing in the list of references matches that particular citation, add a lower-case letter extension to each of the citations. Let's say John Jones wrote three books in 1993. Cite the first one as "1993a," as shown in Figure 42. Label Jones' succeeding references "b," "c," etc., in the order of their citation in the text.

In PCs TODAY, Jones (1993a) states that....

or

Jones (1993a) states that....

or

As society continues to undergo rapid technological change, people suffer from what Toffler calls "future shock" (Jones, 1993a, p. 24).

or

By the year 2000, 95% of all offices will use PCs (Jones, 1993a, pp. 24-25).

Figure 42. Examples of a Citation of a Publication by an Author With More Than One Publication in the Same Year.

Citing a Personal Communication

You may interview an expert or other relevant person face-to-face or by telephone during the course of your research, or you may receive a fax, letter, or E-mail from that person. If you use any portion of these communications, you must cite them in the text. Figure 43 shows an example of a citation for these sources. Give both the initials and the last name of the person involved. Use the words "personal communication" for all of these types of communications.

NOTE: These sources are *not* cited in the reference list because they do not provide recoverable data.

According to J. D. Smith (personal communication,

November 15, 1995), management style . . . .

or

(J. D. Smith, personal communication, November 15,

1995)

Figure 43. Examples of a Citation of a Personal Communication.

Citing Legal Material

Your citations may include legal material. Legal material falls into eight categories:

- Court cases

- Statutes

- Testimony at hearings

- Full hearings

- Unenacted federal bills and resolutions

- Enacted bills and resolutions,

- Federal reports and documents

- Adminstrative and executive materials

Just like books and magazine articles, you must cite legal material in the text; however, it is documented in a slightly different way.

Citing Court Cases

You can cite several types of court cases:

- Court decisions

- Unpublished cases

- Court cases at the trial level

- Court cases at the appellate level

All court cases are cited in the same manner, as shown in Figure 44. Be sure to underline the case title. Note that "v." is used, not the word "versus" or the abbreviation "vs.," and that the "v" is lower case.

The case of <u>Smith v. Jones</u> (1992) set a major legal precedent regarding sexual harrassment in the workplace.

or

Apple Computer Company charged Microsoft Corporation with patent infringement, saying that Microsoft appropriated the code for their graphic interface and used it in their development of their Windows program (<u>Apple Computer v. Microsoft</u>, 1993).

Figure 44. Examples of a Citation of a Court Decision in the Text.

Citing a Statute

When you cite a statute in the text, you must give the:

- name of the act

- year it was passed

You can do this in two ways, as shown in Figure 45. Be sure to use initial caps on each word of the statute.

To prevent people with disabilities from being discriminated against in the workplace and in society at large, the U.S. Congress passed the Americans With Disabilities Act (1990).

or

To prevent people with disabilities from being discriminated against in the workplace and in society at large, the U.S. Congress passed the Americans With Disabilities Act of 1990.

Figure 45. Examples of a Citation of a Statute in the Text.

Citing Testimony at Hearings

When you cite testimony from a hearing in the text of your document, you must:

- indicate that it is testimony

- include the name of the person testifying

- include the year in which the testimony took place

Figure 46 shows two examples. Note that the words "Testimony of John Smith" are underlined.

```
As stated in the Testimony of John Smith (1990), ut wisi

enim ad minim veniam, quis nostrud exerci tation

ullamcorper suscipit lobortis nisl ut aliquip.
```

or

```
"Lorem ipsum dolor sit amet, consectetuer adipiscing

elit, sed diam nonummy nibh euismod tin cidunt ut laoreet

dolore magna aliquam erat volutpat"  (Testimony of John

Smith, 1990).
```

Figure 46. Examples of a Citation of Testimony at a Hearing.

Citing a Full Hearing

When you cite information from a full hearing in the text of your document, you must include the:

- name of the hearing

- year in which the hearing took place

Figure 47 shows two examples.

Note that the title of the hearing is underlined.

In the hearing <u>RU486: The Import Ban and Its Effect on Medical Research</u> (1990), ut wisi enim ad minim veniam, quis nostrud exerci tation ullamcorper suscipit lobortis nisl ut aliquip.

---

or

Lorem ipsum dolor sit amet, consectetuer adipiscing elit, sed diam nonummy nibh euismod tin cidunt ut laoreet dolore magna aliquam erat volutpat (<u>RU486: The Import Ban and Its Effect on Medical Research</u>, 1990).

Figure 47. Examples of a Citation of a Full Hearing.

Citing Unenacted Federal Bills and Resolutions

When you cite an unenacted federal bill or resolution in the text of your document, you must include the:

- name of the bill or resolution

- year in which the bill or resolution was introduced

Figure 48 shows two examples. The title of the hearing is underlined. When the citation is completely within the parentheses, as shown in the second example in Figure 48, only the initials are used and there is a space between the "H." and the "J."

NOTE: The correct abbreviation for a House Joint Resolution, when used in parentheses, is "H. J. Res."

```
House Joint Resolution 504 (1986), introduced by Rep.

Robert Badham, the Republican congressman from Newport

Beach, California, sought to authorize establishment

of a memorial in Washington, DC, or its environs to

honor the Challenger astronauts.
```

or

```
In 1986, Congressman Robert Badham of Newport Beach,

California, sought to pass a resolution authorizing the

building of a memorial to the Challenger astronauts on

federal land in the District of Columbia or its environs

(H. J. Res. 504, 1986).
```

Figure 48. Examples of a Citation of an Unenacted Federal Bill or Resolution.

Citing Enacted Federal Bills and Resolutions

When you cite an enacted federal bill or resolution in the text of your document, you must include the:

- name of the bill or resolution

- year in which the bill or resolution was passed

Bear in mind that enacted federal bills and resolutions are really laws, and, therefore, should be cited as statutes, if possible (see page 78).

Figure 49 shows two examples.

When the citation is completely within the parentheses, as shown in the second example in Figure 49, only the initials are used and there is a space between the "S." and the "B."

NOTE: The correct abbreviation for a Senate Resolution when used in parentheses is "S. Res."

Lorem ipsum dolor sit amet, consectetuer adipiscing elit,
sed diam nonummy nibh euismod tin cidunt ut laoreet
dolore magna aliquam erat volutpat as stated in Senate
Bill 345 (1993).

or

Ut wisi enim ad minim veniam, quis nostrud exerci tation
ullamcorper suscipit lobortis nisl ut aliquip ex ea
commodo consequat (S. B. 345, 1993).

Figure 49. Examples of a Citation of an Enacted Bill or Resolution.

Citing Federal Reports and Documents

When you cite a federal report or document in the text of your document, you must include the:

- number of the report or document

- year in which the report or document was issued

Figure 50 shows two examples.

When using the citation as part of your text, as shown in the first example in Figure 50, the words of the title are completely spelled out, with the exception of "Number," which is abbreviated as "No."

When the citation is completely within the parentheses, as shown in the second example in Figure 50, all the words of the title are abbreviated.

NOTE: The correct abbreviation for a federal document, when used in parentheses, is "Doc"; i.e., (S. Doc. No. 1234, 1992).

Lorem ipsum dolor sit amet, consectetuer adipiscing

elit, sed diam nonummy nibh euismod tin cidunt ut

laoreet dolore magna aliquam erat volutpat as stated

in Senate Report No. 123 (1991).

or

Ut wisi enim ad minim veniam, quis nostrud exerci

tation ullamcorper suscipit lobortis nisl ut aliquip

ex ea commodo consequat (S. Rep. No. 123, 1991).

Figure 50. Examples of a Citation of a Federal Report or Document.

Citing Administrative and Executive Materials

There are two types of administrative and executive materials:

- Federal rules and regulations

- Executive orders and advisory opinions

Citing a Federal Rule or Regulation

You'll find federal rules and regulations in both the *Code of Federal Regulations* and in the *Federal Register.* They are generally published first in the *Federal Register,* then codified in the *Code of Federal Regulations.*

When you cite a federal rule or regulation in the text of your document, you must include the:

- title of the rule or regulation

- year in which the rule or regulation was passed

Figure 51 shows two examples.

NOTE: If the rule is contained in both the *Code* and the *Register,* cite the title from both sources. Put the title of the second citation in parentheses as a cross-reference.

Lorem ipsum dolor sit amet, consectetuer adipiscing elit, sed diam nonummy nibh euismod tin cidunt ut laoreet dolore magna aliquam erat volutpat as stated in the FTC Credit Practices Rule (1991).

or

Ut wisi enim ad minim veniam, quis nostrud exerci tation ullamcorper suscipit lobortis nisl ut aliquip ex ea commodo consequat (FTC Credit Practices Rule, 1991).

Figure 51. Examples of a Citation of a Federal Regulation.

Citing an Executive Order or Advisory Opinion

You'll find executive orders in Volume 3 of the *Code of Federal Regulations*. They may also be listed in the United States Code (U.S.C.).

When you cite an executive order or advisory opinion in the text of your document, you must include the:

- title (which includes the number) of the order or opinion

- year in which the rule or regulation was passed

If the executive order is contained in both the *Code of Federal Regulations* and the United States Code, cite the title from both sources. Put the title of the second citation in parentheses as a cross-reference.

Figure 52 shows two examples.

Lorem ipsum dolor sit amet, consectetuer adipiscing elit, sed diam nonummy nibh euismod tin cidunt ut laoreet dolore magna aliquam erat volutpat as stated in Executive Order No. 12804, 1992).

or

Ut wisi enim ad minim veniam, quis nostrud exerci tation ullamcorper suscipit lobortis nisl ut aliquip ex ea commodo consequat (Executive Order No. 12804, 1992).

Figure 52. Examples of a Citation of an Executive Order.

Chapter 6

Formatting the Frontis Material and Appendices

This chapter explains how to format the frontis material and the appendices of your report, thesis, or research project.

Formatting the Frontis Material

The frontis material of a report, thesis, or research project consists of the:

- title page

- executive summary (optional)

- table of contents

- list of figures

- list of tables

- dedication page (thesis or research project only)

Formatting a Report or Article Title Page

Figure 53 shows a sample of a report or article title page formatted according to APA requirements. It contains the following elements:

- Page header

- Title of report

- Author's name

- College or university name

Center your title page text, leaving lots of white space on either side. Note that all the elements are doublespaced.

Your college or university may wish you to include other elements on the title page. For instance, the University of Phoenix requires its students to include the following:

- Group number

- Name of the class for which the report is being submitted

- Date

Check with your instructor to find out these additional elements or whether you are supposed to use another format altogether.

NOTE: The University of Phoenix business research project and nursing administration project require a different title page format. For the business research project format, see page 94. For the nursing administration project page, see page 96.

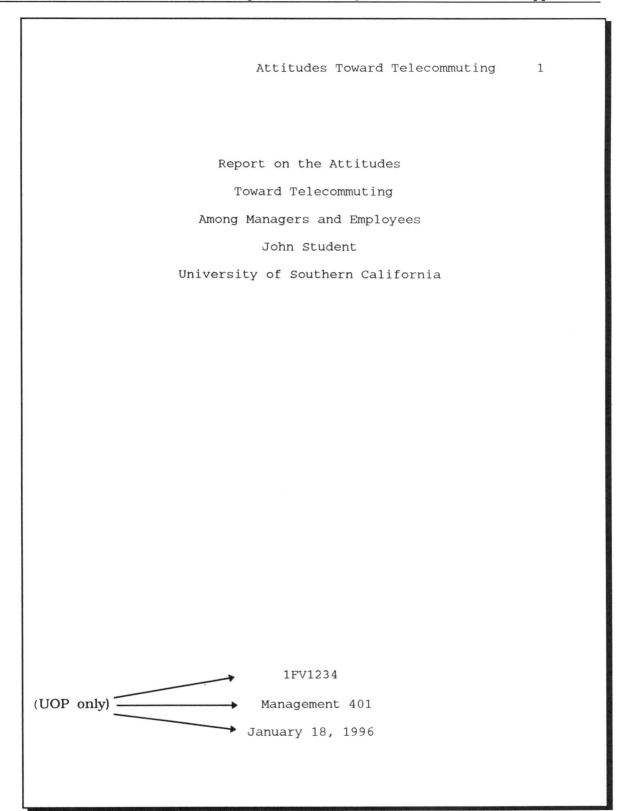

Attitudes Toward Telecommuting   1

                    Report on the Attitudes

                    Toward Telecommuting

                Among Managers and Employees

                        John Student

            University of Southern California

                        1FV1234

(UOP only)   Management 401

                    January 18, 1996

Figure 53. Example of an APA-formatted Report or Article Title Page.

Formatting a Thesis or Project Title Page

This section shows how to format a thesis or project title page. The examples shown here are for the University of Phoenix Business and Nursing Administration Projects. Check with your instructor to find out the specific format for your class or college; if there are no particular requirements, you can base your title page on the examples given.

Formatting a Thesis or Business Research Project Title Page

Figure 54 shows a sample of a UOP business research project title page. This title page contains the following elements:

- Title of project

- Author's name

- Submission paragraph

- Date

Center your title page text, leaving lots of white space on either side. Although no APA rules exist for how much space to include between the elements on the page, UOP students must follow the rules as shown in Figure 54 regarding single- or double-spacing the elements. Every college has its own rules. Check with your instructor. In addition, be sure to type your title in capital letters, and the rest of the elements in initial cap-lower case.

A RESEARCH STUDY TO DETERMINE THE EFFECT

OF THE REORGANIZATION AT XYZ COMPANY

ON EMPLOYEES AND MANAGERS

by

Judy Student

A research project report

submitted to the faculty of

the University of Phoenix

in partial fulfillment

of the requirements for the degree of

Bachelor of Arts in Management

March, 1994

Figure 54. Example Business Research Project Title Page.

Formatting a Nursing Administration Project Title Page

Figure 55 shows an example of a UOP Nursing Administration project title page. This title page contains the following elements:

- Title in capital letters

- Presentation paragraph

- Author's name

- Research faculty member's name

- Statistics faculty member's name

- Group number

- Date

Center your title page text, leaving lots of white space on either side. Although no APA rules exist for how much space to include between the elements on the page, UOP students must follow the rules as shown in Figure 55 regarding single- or double-spacing the elements. Every college has its own rules. Check with your instructor. In addition, be sure to type your title in capital letters, and the rest of the elements in initial cap-lower case.

A RESEARCH STUDY TO DETERMINE

THE EFFECTIVENESS OF COMPUTERIZED MONITORS

ON PATIENTS AND NURSES

AT GENERAL MEDICAL CENTER

A Nursing Administration Project presented
to the faculty of the University of Phoenix
in partial fulfillment of the requirements
for the degree of Masters in Nursing
Administration (MNA)

by

Jane Student

(Research Faculty Member's Name)

(Statistics Faculty Member's Name)

1FV0000

March, 1994

Figure 55. Example Nursing Administration Project Title Page.

Formatting an Executive Summary

If you are a business student, you may be required to include an executive summary in your document. The executive summary is short (approximately one page for reports, two pages for a thesis or project) that includes all the pertinent information that any executive needs to understand exactly what you have studied, concluded, and recommended. It should be jargon-free.

The executive summary is doublespaced, with the words "Executive Summary" at the top per the example of a first page shown in Figure 56.

NOTE: The words "Executive Summary" should be in the same style as the first level heading of your document.

Reorganization Factors   2

EXECUTIVE SUMMARY

Lorem ipsum dolor sit amet, consectetuer adipisci elit, sed diam nonummy nibh eusmod tin cidunt ut loreet dolore magna aliquam erat volutpat. Ut wisi ad minim veniam, quis nostrud exerci tation ulcorper suscipit lobortis nisl ut aliquip ex ea commodo consequat.

Duis atem vel eum iriure dolor in hendrerit in putate velit esse molestie consequat, vel illum dolore feugiat nulla facilisis at vero eros et accumsan et odio dignissim qui blandit praesent luptatum zzril del augue duis dolore te feugait nulla facilisi.

Nam liber tempor cum soluta nobis eleifend id congue nihil imperdiet doming id quod mazim placerat possim assum.

Lorem ipsum dolor sit amet, consectetuer adipisci elit, sed diam nonummy nibh euismod tin cidunt ut loreet dolore magna aliquam erat volutpat. Ut wisi enim minim veniam, quis nostrud exerci tation ullamcorper odio et

Figure 56. Example of the First Page of an Executive Summary.

Formatting a Table of Contents

The Table of Contents is the roadmap by which your readers navigate through your document. The Table of Contents should contain all the headings in the body, worded exactly the same way; therefore, the Table of Contents should not contain any headings that are not in the document.

Some colleges or universities may require that the Table of Contents include the headings, figures and tables in one list in the exact sequence as they appear in the text; ask your instructor. Since most do institutions do not, however, this section presents the table of contents as a standalone item. (See pages 102 and 104 for instructions on how to create a List of Figures and List of Tables.)

Create the Table of Contents after your document is done. Many word processors have an automatic table of contents generator.

Figure 57 shows a sample first page of a Table of Contents for a University of Phoenix Business Research Project. A Table of Contents for a report will be much shorter, of course. Be sure to include all the appendices in the listing. Note that the title, Table of Contents, is not included in the Table of Contents itself, nor are the titles of any of the frontis material; rather, the Table of Contents starts with the body of the document.

NOTE: The words "Table of Contents" should be in the same style as the first level heading of your document.

Reorganization Factors   3

Table of Contents

Figure 57. Example of a Table of Contents.

Formatting a List of Figures

Strict APA guidelines require that you include your figures in the regular Table of Contents. Once again, this requirement is for publication purposes in the *APA Journal.* Most professors wish a separate list of figures, however. This section shows you how to format such a list.

Just as the Table of Contents acts as a roadmap to guide your readers through the text of your document, the List of Figures is a roadmap to the drawings and pictures your document contains. In other words, it is the "table of contents" for your figures. Create a List of Figures if you have three or more figures in your document.

If your word processor has an automatic table of contents generator that will generate the List of Figures, use that. If you do not have too many figures, it may be just as easy to create the list by hand.

Figure 58 shows a sample List of Figures. Yours may be as long as necessary.

NOTE: The words "List of Figures" should be in the same style as the first level heading of your document.

Reorganization Factors   5

List of Figures

Figure 58. Example of a List of Figures.

Formatting a List of Tables

Strict APA guidelines require that you include your tables in the regular Table of Contents. Once again, this requirement is for publication purposes in the *APA Journal*. Most professors wish a separate list of tables, however. This section shows you how to format such a list.

Just as the Table of Contents acts as a roadmap to guide your readers through the text of your document and the List of Figures is a roadmap to the drawings and pictures, the List of Tables is a roadmap to the tables in your document. In other words, it is the "table of contents" for your tables. Create a List of Tables if you have three or more tables in your document.

If your word processor has an automatic table of contents generator that will generate the List of Tables, use that. If you do not have too many tables, it may be just as easy to create the list by hand.

Figure 59 shows a sample List of Tables. Yours may be as long as necessary.

NOTE: The words "List of Tables" should be in the same style as the 1st level heading of your document.

Reorganization Factors   6

List of Tables

Figure 59. Example of a List of Tables.

Formatting a Dedication Page

> *NOTE:*   *This information applies to theses, projects, and dissertations only.*

The dedication page provides an opportunity to thank people who have been a tremendous help to you in getting your project done. Generally, a work is not dedicated to professional colleagues, but to family members who have sacrificed to give you the time you needed to complete it. While a dedication is not a requirement, it is a nice gesture.

Figure 60 shows a sample of a dedication page.

Reorganization Factors   7

Dedication

This project is dedicated to my
wonderful husband, Jim, and my
children, Stacy and Jeff, without whose understanding and great
sacrifices I could not have
completed it.

Figure 60. Example of a Dedication Page.

Formatting the Appendices

If you have only one appendix, just call it "Appendix." If you have two or more appendices, however, call them Appendix A, Appendix B, and so on. Include a title with each appendix.

Strict APA style requires that you place the appendix letter and title on the first page of the material in the appendix. Your college or university, however, may wish you to create a separate title page for each one. Figure 61 shows an example of such a separate appendix title page. Include your information behind this title page.

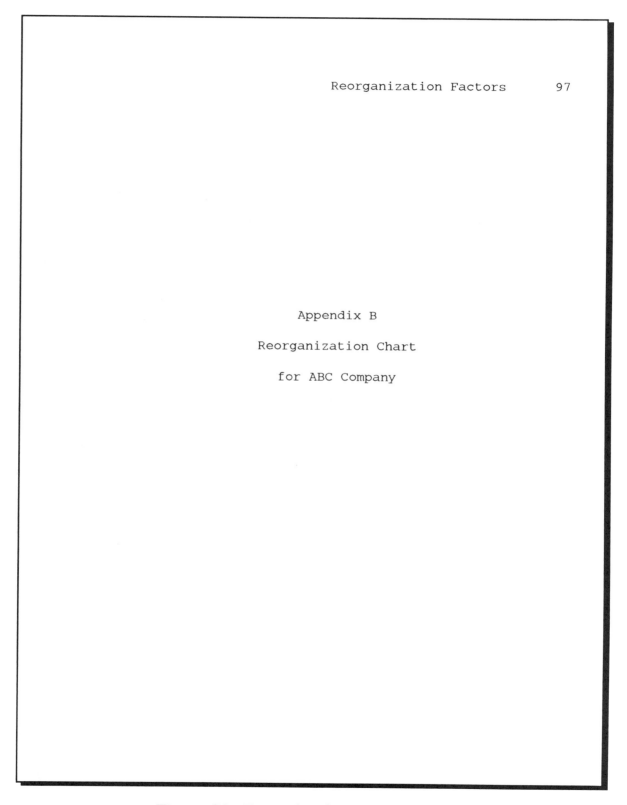

Reorganization Factors   97

Appendix B

Reorganization Chart

for ABC Company

Figure 61. Example of an Appendix Title Page.

Numbering the Pages

As explained on page 26, number the pages of your document chronologically starting with the title page. This includes the frontis material and the appendices.

As a reminder, Table 14 shows how to number the pages of your document.

Table 14. Correct Page Numbering.

PAGES	STYLE OF NUMBER	STARTING NUMBER
Title page	None or arabic numeral	1
Executive Summary	Arabic numeral(s)	2
Table of Contents	Arabic numeral(s)	2 or number following the Executive Summary
List of Figures	Arabic numeral(s)	Number following the Table of Contents
List of Tables	Arabic numeral(s)	Number following the List of Figures
Body	Arabic numerals	Number following the Table of Contents or List of Figures or Tables, whichever is last
Appendices	Arabic numeral(s)	Number following the last page of the body

Numbering Figures and Tables in the Appendices

When you number figures and tables in the appendices, you must include the appendix letter in the numbering; i.e., Figure A1, Figure A2, Figure B1, Figure B2, Table A1, Table B1, etc. Once again, the lists of figures and tables must be separate.

Chapter 7

Creating a Bibliography or List of References

What is the difference between a bibliography and a list of references? Strictly speaking, a bibliography is a list of books ("biblio" is from the Greek word *biblion*, meaning book, and "-graphy" is the combining form meaning a writing—from the Greek word *graphein*, to write). A list of references can include references not only from books, but also from other sources, such as magazines, journals, newspapers, company documents, etc.

The APA defines the difference between a bibliography and a list of references a little differently. A list of references includes the works cited in a particular document. A bibliography, on the other hand, lists works for further reading or for background information, and each work cited may include a brief blurb describing the contents. The APA style guide requires reference lists, not bibliographies.

This chapter shows you how to reference:

- journal articles

- magazine articles

- newsletter articles

- newspaper articles

- monographs

- abstracts

- company brochures

- personal interviews and correspondence

- encyclopedias or dictionaries

- government publications

- academic material

- raw data

- book, movie, and video reviews

- audio-visual media

- electronic media

- legal materials

Follow these rules when creating references:

- Place the word "References" at the top of the list.

- Create the list in alphabetical order by the author's last name.

- Follow the layout and punctuation exactly as shown in this chapter.

NOTE: Many of the examples shown in this section are not real, but have been created for example purposes.

For an example list of references, please see Appendix F.

Referencing Periodicals

This section shows you how to reference:

- journal articles

- magazine articles

- newsletters

- newspapers

- monographs

- abstracts

- periodicals published annually

- works discussed in secondary sources

Referencing Journal Articles

When you reference a journal article, you must reference both the article and the journal it is in. This section shows you how to reference a(n):

- journal article with one author

- journal article with two authors

- journal article with three to five authors

- journal article with six or more authors

- journal article in press

- entire issue of a journal

- journal supplement

- non-English journal article with the title translated into English

- English translation of a journal article

Referencing a Journal Article With One Author

A reference for a journal article with one author appears as shown in Figure 62 and consists of the following elements:

- Author's last name

- Author's first initial and middle initial, if available

- Year of journal issue

- Title of article

- Title of journal

- Volume (and issue) number, if available

- Page number(s) of article

To create this reference, follow these steps:

1. Indent one-half inch and type the author's last name in full, followed by a comma and a space.

2. Type the author's first initial (*not* the full first name), followed by a period and a space, then the middle initial (if available), followed by a period and a space. If the author's middle name is not listed, just use the first initial.

Remember: Never, never use the full first name!

3. Type the copyright year in parentheses, followed by a period and a space.

4. Type the title of the article in plain type. Use a capital letter on the first word, but use lower-case letters on the remaining words. End with a period and a space.

5. Type the journal title. Capitalize all words, and follow it with a comma, a space, and the volume number, if available. Underline the title and the volume number. (If the issue number is available, place it in parentheses and follow it with a comma, as shown).

6. Type a space and the page numbers, followed by a period.

    NOTE: Notice that the "pp." is not included in the page number shown in Figure 62. The "p." or "pp." is not used when the volume number is included.

7. If your reference continues to a second line, doublespace the second line and begin it back at the left margin.

Follow this format exactly. See Appendix F for a complete list of references.

Matthews, Y. A. (1993). Electronic communication in large organizations. <u>Technical Communication, 39</u>(2), 60-65.

Figure 62. Example of a Reference of a Journal Article With One Author.

Referencing a Journal Article With Two Authors

A reference for a journal article with two authors appears as shown in Figure 63 and consists of the following elements:

- Both authors' last names

- Both authors' first initials

- Year of journal issue

- Title of article

- Title of journal

- Volume (and issue) number, if available

- Page number(s) of article

To create this reference, follow these steps:

1. Indent one-half inch and type the first author's last name in full, followed by a comma and a space.

2. Type the first author's first initial (*not* the full first name), followed by a period, a comma, and a space.

Remember: Never, never use the full first name!

3. Type an ampersand (&) and a space.

4. Type the second author's last name, followed by a comma and a space.

5. Type the second author's first initial, followed by a period and a space.

6. Type the copyright year in parentheses, followed by a period and a space.

7. Type the title of the article in plain type. Use a capital letter on the first word, but use lower-case letters on the remaining words. End the title with a period and a space.

8. Type the journal title. Capitalize all words of the title, and follow it with a comma, a space, and the volume number, if available. Underline the title and the volume number. (If the issue number is available, place it in parentheses and follow it with a comma, as shown in Figure 63.)

9. Type a space and the page numbers, followed by a period.

   NOTE: Notice that the "pp." is not included in the page number shown in Figure 63. The "p." or "pp." is not used when the volume number is included.

10. If your reference continues to a second line, doublespace the second line and begin it back at the left margin.

Follow this format exactly. See Appendix F for a complete list of references.

Matthews, Y., & Jones, T. (1993). Electronic communication in large organizations. Technical Communication, 39(2), 60-65.

Figure 63. Example of a Reference of a Journal Article With Two Authors.

Referencing a Journal Article With Three to Five Authors

A reference for a journal article with three to five authors appears as shown in Figure 64 and consists of the following elements:

- Authors' last names

- Authors' first initials and middle initials, if available

- Year of journal issue

- Title of article

- Title of journal

- Volume (and issue) number, if available

- Page number(s) of article

To create this reference, follow these steps:

1. Indent one-half inch and type the first author's last name in full, followed by a comma and a space.

2. Type the first author's first initial (*not* the full first name), followed by a period and a space, then the middle initial, if available, a period, a comma, and a space.

Remember: Never, never use the full first name!

3. Type the second author's last name in full, followed by a comma and a space.

4. Repeat Step 3 for all authors except the last.

5. After the next-to-the-last author's middle initial, type an ampersand (&) and a space.

6. Type the last author's last name, followed by a comma and a space.

7. Type the last author's first initial, followed by a period and a space, then the middle initial, if available, followed by a period and a space.

8. Type the copyright year in parentheses, followed by a period and a space.

9. Type the title of the article in plain type. Use a capital letter on the first word, but use lower-case letters on the remaining words. End the title with a period and a space.

10. Type the journal title. Capitalize all words of the title, and follow it with a comma, a space, and the volume number, if available. Underline the title and the volume number. (If the issue number is available, place it in parentheses and follow it with a comma, as shown in Figure 64.)

11. Type a space and the page numbers, followed by a period.

     NOTE: Notice that the "pp." is not included in the page number shown in Figure 64. The "p." or "pp." is not used when the volume number is included.

12. If your reference continues to a second line, doublespace the second line and begin it back at the left margin.

Follow this format exactly. See Appendix F for a complete list of references.

Ridgeway, L. S., Grice, R. A., & Gould, E. (1992). I'm ok, you're only a user. Technical Communication, 39 (1), 38-49.

Figure 64. Example of a Reference of a Journal Article With Three to Five Authors.

Referencing a Journal Article With Six or More Authors

A reference for a journal article with six or more authors appears as shown in Figure 65 and consists of the following elements:

- Authors' last names

- Authors' first initials and middle initials, if available

- Year of journal issue

- Title of article

- Title of journal

- Volume (and issue) number, if available

- Page number(s) of article

To create this reference, follow these steps:

1. Indent one-half inch and type the first author's last name in full, followed by a comma and a space.

2. Type the first author's first initial (*not* the full first name), followed by a period and a space, then the middle initial, if available, a period, a comma, and a space.

Remember: Never, never use the full first name!

3. Type the second author's last name in full, followed by a comma and a space.

4. Type the second author's first initial (*not* the full first name), followed by a period and a space, then the middle initial, if available, a period, a comma, and a space.

5. Repeat Steps 3 and 4 for all remaining authors except the last.

6. Type an ampersand (&) and a space.

7. Type the last author's last name, followed by a comma and a space.

8. Type the second author's first initial (*not* the full first name), followed by a period and a space, then the middle initial, if available, followed by a period and a space.

9. Type the copyright year in parentheses, followed by a period and a space.

10. Type the title of the article in plain type. Use a capital letter on the first word, but use lower-case letters on the remaining words. End with a period and a space.

   EXCEPTION: Note that the word "You're" has a capital "Y" because it is the first word of the subtitle.

11. Type the journal title. Capitalize all words of the title, and follow it with a comma, a space, and the volume number, if available. Underline the title and the volume number. (If the issue number is available, place it in parentheses and follow it with a comma, as shown in Figure 65.)

12. Type a space and the page numbers, followed by a period.

   NOTE: Notice that the "pp." is not included in the page number shown in Figure 65. The "p." or "pp." is not used when the volume number is included.

13. If your reference continues to a second line, doublespace the second line and begin it back at the left margin.

Follow this format exactly. See Appendix F for a complete list of references.

```
Ridgeway, L. S., Grice, R. A., Jones, T., Cruz, A.,

Washington, K., & Gould, E. (1992).  I'm ok; You're only

a user. Technical Communication, 39(1), 38-49.
```

Figure 65. Example of a Reference of a Journal Article With Six or More Authors.

Referencing a Journal Article In Press

You may reference an article that has been accepted for publication, but the journal has not yet been published. This article is then "in press." Let's say it has one author. A reference for a journal article in press with one author appears as shown in Figure 66 and consists of the following elements:

- Author's last name

- Author's first initial and middle initial, if available

- Title of article

- Title of journal

To create this reference, follow these steps:

1. Indent one-half inch and type the author's last name in full, followed by a comma and a space.

2. Type the author's first initial (*not* the full first name), followed by a period and a space, then the middle initial, if available, followed by a period and a space. If the author's middle name is not listed, just use the first initial.

Remember: Never, never use the full first name!

3. Type the title of the article in plain type. Use a capital letter on the first word, but use lower-case letters on the remaining words. End the title with a period and a space.

4. Type the journal title. Capitalize all words of the title, and follow it with a comma, a space, and the volume number, if available. Underline the title.

NOTE: The year, volume, issue, and page numbers are not included because the article has not yet been published.

5. If your reference continues to a second line, doublespace the second line and begin it back at the left margin.

Follow this format exactly. See Appendix F for a complete list of references.

NOTE: If the article has more than one author, follow the
rules for that number of authors.

```
    Fye, W. B. The origin of the full-time faculty

system. Journal of Education.
```

Figure 66. Example of a Reference of a Journal Article in Press.

NOTE: In the text, cite the article as follows:

```
        (Author's last name, in press)
```

Referencing an Entire Issue of a Journal

A reference for an entire issue of a journal appears as shown in Figure 67 and consists of the following elements:

- Editor's last name

- Editor's first initial and middle initial, if available

- The abbreviation "Ed."

- Year of journal issue

- Title of journal issue

- The words "Special issue"

- Title of journal

- Volume (and issue) number, if available

To create this reference, follow these steps:

1. Indent one-half inch and type the editor's last name in full, followed by a comma and a space.

2. Type the editor's first initial, followed by a period and a space, then the middle initial (if available), followed by a period and a space. If the editor's middle name is not listed, just use the first initial.

Remember: Never, never use the full first name!

3. Type the abbreviation "Ed." in parentheses, followed by a period and a space.

4. Type the copyright year in parentheses, followed by a period and a space.

5. Type the special issue title in plain type. Use a capital letter on the first word, but use lower-case letters on the remaining words. Follow this with a period and a space.

6. Type "Special issue" in brackets, followed by a period and a space. Capitalize the "S" on "special.."

7. Type the journal title. Capitalize all words of the title, and follow it with a comma, a space, and the volume number, if available. Underline the title and the volume number. (If the issue number is available, place it in parentheses). Follow the information with a period.

8. If your reference continues to a second line, doublespace the second line and begin it back at the left margin.

Follow this format exactly. See Appendix F for a complete list of references.

Shelton, S. M. (Ed.). (1991). Visual communication [Special issue]. Technical Communication, 40(4).

Figure 67. Example of a Reference of an Entire Issue of a Journal.

Referencing a Journal Supplement

A reference for a journal supplement appears as shown in Figure 68 and consists of the following elements:

- Author's last name

- Author's first initial and middle initial, if available

- Year of journal issue

- Title of journal

- Title of journal

- Volume (and issue) number, if available

- The abbreviation "Suppl." and the supplement number

- Page numbers

To create this reference, follow these steps:

1. Indent one-half inch and type the author's last name in full, followed by a comma and a space.

2. Type the author's first initial, followed by a period and a space, then the middle initial (if available), followed by a period, a comma, and a space. If the author's middle name is not listed, just use the first initial.

Remember: Never, never use the full first name!

3. Type the copyright year in parentheses, followed by a period and a space.

4. Type the title of the journal in plain type. Use a capital letter on the first word, but use lower-case letters on the remaining words. Type a space.

5. Type the journal title. Capitalize all words of the title, and follow it with a comma, a space, and the volume number, if available. Underline the title and the volume number.

6. Immediately following the volume number, in parentheses, put the abbreviation "Suppl," followed by a period and a space, and then the supplement number.

7. After the closing parenthesis, type a space and then the page numbers (do not use "p." or "pp.").

8. If your reference continues to a second line, doublespace the second line and begin it back at the left margin.

Follow this format exactly. See Appendix F for a complete list of references.

```
    Shelton, S. M. (Ed.). (1991). Visual communication

Technical Communication, 40(Suppl. 4) 18-24.
```

Figure 68. Example of a Reference of a Journal Supplement.

Referencing a Non-English Journal Article With the Title Translated into English

A reference for a non-English journal article with the title translated into English appears as shown in Figure 69 and consists of the following elements:

- Author's last name

- Author's first initial and middle initial, if available

- Copyright year of journal

- Original title of article

- Title of article in English

- Title of journal

- Volume (and issue) number, if available

- Page numbers

To create this reference, follow these steps:

1. Indent one-half inch and type the author's last name in full, followed by a comma.

2. Type the author's first initial, followed by a period and a space, then the middle initial (if available), followed by a period, a comma, and a space. If the author's middle name is not listed, just use the first initial.

Remember: Never, never use the full first name!

3. Type the copyright year in parentheses, followed by a period and a space.

4. Type the original title of the article in plain type. Use a capital letter on the first word, but use lower-case letters on the remaining words, unless they are proper nouns. (In German, all nouns are capitalized; therefore, they are capitalized in Figure 69). Include any diacritical marks. After the title, type a space.

5. Type the English title of the article in brackets, followed by a period and a space.

6. Type the journal title. Capitalize all words of the title, and follow it with a comma, a space, and the volume number, if available. Underline the title and the volume number. If the issue number is available, place it in parentheses and follow it with a comma and a space (not shown in Figure 69.)

7. Type the page numbers, followed by a period.

NOTE: Notice that the "pp." is not included in the page number shown in Figure 69. The "p." or "pp." is not used when the volume number is included.

8. If your reference continues to a second line, doublespace the second line and begin it back at the left margin.

Follow this format exactly. See Appendix F for a complete list of references.

Zajonc, R. B. (1989). Bischofs gefühlvolle Verwirrunggen über die Gefühle [Bischof's emotional flare over the emotions]. Psychologische Rundschau, 40, 218-211.

Figure 69. Example of a Reference of a Non-English Journal Article With the Title Translated into English.

Referencing an English Translation of a Journal Article

A reference for an English translation of a journal article appears as shown in Figure 70 and consists of the following elements:

- Author's last name

- Author's first initial

- Copyright year of journal

- English title of article

- Title of journal

- Volume (and issue) number, if available

- Page numbers

To create this reference, follow these steps:

1. Indent one-half inch and type the author's last name in full, followed by a comma and a space.

2. Type the author's first initial, followed by a period and a space.

Remember: Never, never use the full first name!

3. Type the copyright year in parentheses, followed by a period and a space.

4. Type the title of the article in plain type, followed by a period and a space. Use a capital letter on the first word, but use lower-case letters on the remaining words.

5. Type the journal title. Capitalize all words of the title, and follow it with a comma, a space, and the volume number, if available. Underline the title and the volume number. If the issue number is available, place it in parentheses and follow it with a comma.

6. Type a space and the page numbers, followed by a period.

NOTE: Notice that the "pp." is not included in the page number shown in Figure 70. The "p." or "pp." is not used when the volume number is included.

7. Type the page numbers.

8. If your reference continues to a second line, doublespace the second line and begin it back at the left margin.

Follow this format exactly. See Appendix F for a complete list of references.

Zajonc, R. (1989). Bischof's emotional flare

over the emotions. Psychologische Rundschau, 40, 218-211.

Figure 70. Example of a Reference of an English Translation of a Journal Article.

Referencing Magazine Articles

This section shows you how to reference a:

- magazine article with an author

- magazine article with no author

Referencing a Magazine Article With An Author

When you reference a magazine article with an author, you must reference both the article and the magazine it is in. A reference for a magazine article with an author appears as shown in Figure 71 and consists of the following elements:

- Author's last name

- Author's first initial and middle initial, if available

- Year, month, (and day, if applicable) of magazine issue

- Title of article

- Title of magazine

- Volume number, if available

- Page number(s) of article

To create this reference, follow these steps:

1. Indent one-half inch and type the author's last name in full, followed by a comma and a space.

2. Type the author's first initial (*not* the full first name), followed by a period and a space, then the middle initial (if available), followed by a period and a space. If the author's middle name is not listed, just use the first initial.

Remember: Never, never use the full first name!

3. Type the copyright year in parentheses, followed by a comma, a space, the month of publication (and the day, too, if applicable (i.e., June 15)), a period, and a space.

4. Type the title of the article in plain type. Use a capital letter on the first word, but use lower-case letters on the remaining words. End the title with a period and a space.

5. Type the magazine title. Capitalize all words of the title, and follow it with a comma, a space, and the volume number, if available, and another comma. Underline the title and the volume number.

6. Type a space and the page numbers, followed by a period.

   NOTE: Notice that the "pp." is not included in the page number shown in Figure 71. The "p." or "pp." is not used when the volume number is included; therefore, use these initials only when the volume number is not included.

7. If your reference continues to a second line, doublespace the second line and begin it back at the left margin.

Follow this format exactly. See Appendix F for a complete list of references.

Morrison, H. A. (1992, December). The paperless office. <u>Business Talk, 115,</u> 70-76.

Figure 71.   Example of a Reference of a Magazine Article With an Author.

Referencing a Magazine Article With No Author

Many articles are "staff-written"; that is, they are written by someone on the magazine's staff and do not exhibit a byline.

When you reference a magazine article with no author, you must reference both the article and the magazine. An example appears as shown in Figure 72 and consists of the following elements:

- Title of magazine

- Title of article

- Month, (and day, if applicable) and year of magazine issue

- Page number(s) of article

To create this reference, follow these steps:

1. Indent one-half inch and type the magazine title. Follow it with a period and a space. Underline the title and the period.

2. Type the copyright year in parentheses, followed by a comma, a space, and the month of publication (the day, too, if applicable; i.e., June 15), and then a period and a space.

3. Type the article title in plain type. Use a capital letter on the first word, but lower-case letters on the remaining words. End the title with a period.

4. Type "P." (or "Pp.") and the page number(s) followed by a period. The first "p" is capitalized because it begins the sentence.

5. If your reference continues to a second line, doublespace the second line and begin it back at the left margin.

Follow this format exactly. See Appendix F for a complete list of references.

Business Talk. (1992, December). Time management
tips.   Pp. 70-76.

Figure 72. Example of a Reference of a Magazine Article With No Author.

Referencing Newsletter Articles

Referencing a Newsletter Article With an Author

When you reference a newsletter article with an author, you must reference both the article and the newsletter it is in. A reference for a newsletter article with an author appears as shown in Figure 73 and consists of the following elements:

- Author's last name

- Author's first initial and middle initial, if available

- Year, month, (and day, if applicable) (or season) of newletter issue

- Title of article

- Title of newsletter

- Volume number, if available

- Page number(s) of article

To create this reference, follow these steps:

1. Indent one-half inch and type the author's last name in full, followed by a comma and a space.

2. Type the author's first initial (*not* the full first name), followed by a period and a space, then the middle initial (if available), followed by a period and a space. If the author's middle name is not listed, just use the first initial.

Remember: Never, never use the full first name!

3. Type the copyright year in parentheses, followed by a comma, a space, the month of publication (and the day, too, if applicable (i.e., June 15)) or the season, and a period.

4. Type the title of the article in plain type. Use a capital letter on the first word, but use lower-case letters on the remaining words. End the title with a period and a space. (If the title ends with a question mark, as shown in Figure 73, or an exclamation point, do not use a period.)

5. Type the newsletter title. Capitalize all words of the title, and follow it with a comma, a space, and the volume number, if available, and another comma. Underline the title and the volume number.

6. Type a space and the page numbers, followed by a period.

    NOTE: Notice that the "pp." is not included in the page number shown in Figure 73. The "p." or "pp." is not used when the volume number is included.

7. If your reference continues to a second line, doublespace the second line and begin it back at the left margin.

Follow this format exactly. See Appendix F for a complete list of references.

        Jones, L. B. (1994, Spring). Employees or independent

contractors? The Small Business Newsletter, 24, 22-24.

Figure 73. Example of a Reference of a Newsletter Article With an Author.

Referencing a Newsletter Article With No Author

Many articles are "staff-written"; that is, they are written by someone on the newsletter's staff and do not exhibit a byline. When you reference a newsletter article with no author, you must reference both the article and the newsletter. An example appears as shown in Figure 74 and consists of the following elements:

- Title of article

- Year, month, (and day, if applicable) of issue

- Title of newsletter

- Volume number

- Page number(s) of article

To create this reference, follow these steps:

1. Indent one-half inch and type the article title. Use a capital letter on the first word, but lower-case letters on the remaining words. End with a period and a space.

2. Type the copyright year in parentheses, followed by a comma, a space, the month of publication (the day, too, if applicable; i.e., June 15), and then a period and a space.

3. Type the newsletter title, followed by a comma, a space, the volume number, if available, and another comma. Underline the title, the volume number, and the comma.

4. Type the page numbers, followed by a period.

5. If your reference continues to a second line, doublespace the second line and begin it back at the left margin.

Follow this format exactly. See Appendix F for a complete list of references.

The IRS' Section 1706 tax laws. (1992, May). The
Consultant's News, 14, 24-26.

Figure 74. Example of a Reference of a Newsletter Article With No Author.

Referencing Newspaper Articles

This section shows you how to reference a:

- newspaper article with an author

- newspaper article with no author

- letter to the editor

Referencing a Newspaper Article With an Author

Reference a newspaper article with an author just as you would a magazine article with an author. Just put the newspaper's name where the magazine title goes. A reference for a newspaper article appears as shown in Figure 75 and consists of the following elements:

- Author's last name

- Author's first initial and middle initial, if available

- Title of article

- Title of newspaper

- Month, day, and year of newspaper issue

- Page number(s) of article

To create this reference, follow these steps:

1. Indent one-half inch and type the author's last name in full, followed by a comma and a space.

2. Type the author's first initial (*not* the full first name), followed by a period and a space, then the middle initial (if available), followed by a period and a space. If the author's middle name is not listed, just use the first initial.

Remember: Never, never use the full first name!

3. Type the copyright year in parentheses, followed by a comma, a space, the month of publication (the day, too, if applicable; i.e., June 15), and then a period and a space.

4. Type the title of the article in plain type. Use a capital letter on the first word, but use lower-case letters on all the other words. End the title with a period and a space. (If the title ends with a question mark, as shown in Figure 75, or an exclamation point, do not use a period.)

5. Type the newspaper title, then underline it. Capitalize all words of the title and follow it with a comma and a space.

6. Type "p." (or "pp.") and the section letter and page number(s), followed by a period.

   Type discontinous pages in the following format: pp. B1, B3.

7. If your reference continues to a second line, doublespace the second line and begin it back at the left margin.

Follow this format exactly. See Appendix F for a complete list of references.

```
     Jones, J. T. (1993, December 10).   Is an upturn in

California's economy still years away?   Los Angeles

Times, p. B-24.
```

Figure 75.   Example of a Reference of a Newspaper Article With an Author.

Referencing a Newspaper Article With No Author

Just as with magazines, some newspaper articles are staff-written and have no byline credit. A reference for a newspaper article with no author appears as shown in Figure 76 and consists of the following elements:

- Title of article

- Year, month, and day of newspaper issue

- Title of newspaper

- Page number(s) of article

To create this reference, follow these steps:

1. Indent one-half inch, and type the title of the article in plain type. Use a capital letter on the first word, but use lower-case letters on all the other words. End the title with a period and a space. (If the title ends with a question mark, as shown in Figure 76, or an exclamation point, do not use a period.)

2. Type the copyright year in parentheses, followed by a comma, a space, the month of publication (and the day, too, if applicable (i.e., June 15)), and then a period and a space.

3. Type the newspaper title, then underline it. Capitalize all the words of the title and follow it with a comma and a space.

4. Type "p." (or "pp.") and the page number(s), followed by a period. Type discontinuous pages in the following format: B1, B3.

5. If your reference continues to a second line, doublespace the second line and begin it back at the left margin.

Follow this format exactly. See Appendix F for a complete list of references.

Is an upturn in California's economy still years away? (1993, December 10). <u>Los Angeles Times,</u> p. B-24.

Figure 76.   Example of a Reference of a Newspaper Article With No Author.

Referencing a Letter to the Editor

Reference a newspaper article with an author just as you would a magazine article with an author. Just put the newspaper's name where the magazine title goes. A reference for a newspaper article appears as shown in Figure 77 and consists of the following elements:

- Author's last name

- Author's first initial and middle initial, if available

- Title of article

- The phrase "Letter to the Editor"

- Title of newspaper

- Month, day, and year of newspaper issue

- Page number(s) of article

To create this reference, follow these steps:

1. Indent one-half inch and type the author's last name in full, followed by a comma and a space.

2. Type the author's first initial (*not* the full first name), followed by a period and a space, then the middle initial (if available), followed by a period and a space. If the author's middle name is not listed, just use the first initial.

Remember: Never, never use the full first name!

3. Type the copyright year in parentheses, followed by the month of publication (the day, too, if applicable; i.e., June 15), and then a period and a space.

4. Type the title of the article in plain type. Use a capital letter on the first word, but use lower-case letters on all the other words. End with a space.

5. In brackets, type the phrase "Letter to the Editor." Capitalize the "L" on "Letter," and leave the rest of the words lower case. End with a period and a space.

6. Type the newspaper title, then underline it. Capitalize all words of the title and follow it with a comma.

7. Type "p." (or "pp.") and the section letter and page number(s), followed by a period.

   Type discontinous pages in the following format: pp. B1, B3.

8. If your reference continues to a second line, doublespace the second line and begin it back at the left margin.

Follow this format exactly. See Appendix F for a complete list of references.

```
     Jones, J. T. (1993, December 10).   Welfare or

workfare [Letter to the editor]. Los Angeles

Times, p. B-24.
```

Figure 77. Example of a Reference of a Letter to the Editor.

Referencing Monographs

This section shows you how to reference a:

- monograph with issue number and serial (or whole) number

- monograph bound separately as a supplement to a journal

- monograph bound into a journal

Referencing a Monograph With Issue Number and Serial (or Whole) Number

A reference for a monograph with an issue number and serial (or whole) number is shown in Figure 78 and consists of the following elements:

- Author's last name

- Author's first initial and middle initial, if available

- Copyright year

- Title of monograph

- Title of monograph series

- Volume number

- Issue number

- Serial (or whole) number

To create this reference, follow these steps:

1. Indent one-half inch and type the author's last name in full, followed by a comma and a space.

2. Type the author's first initial (*not* the full first name), followed by a period and a space, then the middle initial (if available), followed by a period and a space. If the author's middle name is not listed, just use the first initial.

Remember: Never, never use the full first name!

3. Type the copyright year in parentheses, followed by a period and a space.

4. Type the title of the monograph, followed by a period and a space. Use a capital letter on the first word, but use lower-case letters on all the other words.

5. Type the title of the monograph series, followed by a comma, a space, the volume number, and another comma. Underline all of it. Capitalize all words of the title.

6. Immediately after the volume number, in parentheses, type the issue number, a comma, a space, and the serial number (or the word "Whole" if the monograph is identified by a whole number). End with a period.

7. If your reference continues to a second line, doublespace the second line and begin it back at the left margin.

Follow this format exactly. See Appendix F for a complete list of references.

```
        Smith, H. N. (1992).  Five prehistoric sites

in Orange County, California.  Monographs of the

South County Museum, 18, (2, Serial No. 134).
```

Figure 78. Example of a Reference of a Monograph With Issue Number and Serial (or Whole) Number.

Referencing a Monograph Bound Separately as a Supplement to a Journal

A reference for a monograph bound separately as a supplement to a journal is shown in Figure 79 and consists of the following elements:

- Author's last name

- Author's first initial and middle initial, if available

- Copyright year

- Title of monograph

- Title of monograph series

- Volume number

- Issue number

- The abbreviation "Suppl." or "Pt."

- Supplement or part number

To create this reference, follow these steps:

1. Indent one-half inch and type the author's last name in full, followed by a comma and a space.

2. Type the author's first initial (*not* the full first name), followed by a period and a space, then the middle initial (if available), followed by a period and a space. If the author's middle name is not listed, just use the first initial.

Remember: Never, never use the full first name!

3. Type the copyright year in parentheses, followed by a period and a space.

4. Type the title of the monograph, followed by a period and a space. Use a capital letter on the first word, but use lower-case letters on all the other words.

5. Type the title of the monograph series, followed by a comma, a space, the volume number, and another comma. Then underline all of it. Capitalize all words of the title.

6. Immediately after the volume number, in parentheses, type the issue number, a comma, a space, and the abbreviation "Pt." for "part" (or "Suppl.," if it is a supplement number), a space, and then the part number (or supplement number) itself. End with a period.

7. If your reference continues to a second line, doublespace the second line and begin it back at the left margin.

Follow this format exactly. See Appendix F for a complete list of references.

```
    Smith, H. N. (1992).  Five prehistoric sites

in Orange County, California.  Monographs of the

South County Museum, 18, (2, Pt. 3).
```

Figure 79. Example of a Reference of a Monograph Bound Separately as a Supplement to a Journal.

Referencing a Monograph Bound into a Journal

A reference for a monograph bound into a journal is shown in Figure 80 and consists of the following elements:

- Author's last name

- Author's first initial and middle initial, if available

- Copyright year

- Title of monograph

- The word "Monograph"

- Journal title

- Volume number

- Issue number

- The abbreviation "Suppl." or "Pt."

- Supplement or part number

To create this reference, follow these steps:

1. Indent one-half inch and type the author's last name in full, followed by a comma.

2. Type the author's first initial (*not* the full first name), followed by a period and a space, then the middle initial (if available), followed by a period and a space. If the author's middle name is not listed, just use the first initial.

Remember: Never, never use the full first name!

3. Type the copyright year in parentheses, followed by a period and a space.

4. Type the title of the monograph, followed by a space. Use a capital letter on the first word, but use lower-case letters on all the other words unless they are proper nouns.

5. Type the word "Monograph" in brackets, and follow that with a period.

6. Type the title of the journal, followed by a comma, a space, and the volume number. Underline all of these elements. Capitalize all words of the title.

7. Type a space, and then the page numbers and a period.

   NOTE: Notice that the "pp." is not included in the page number shown in Figure 80. The "p." or "pp." is not used when the volume number is included.

8. If your reference continues to a second line, doublespace the second line and begin it back at the left margin.

Follow this format exactly. See Appendix F for a complete list of references.

```
        Smith, H. N. (1992).   Five prehistoric sites

in Orange County, California [Monograph].   Journal

of the Southwest Archeological Association, 18, 88-125.
```

Figure 80. Example of a Reference of a Monograph Bound into a Journal with Continuous Pagination.

Referencing Abstracts

This section shows you how to reference an:

- abstract an an original source

- abstract from a secondary source

Referencing an Abstract as an Original Source

Sometimes, you will find an abstract that you want to reference as an original source. A reference for an abstract as an original source is shown in Figure 81 and consists of the following elements:

- Author's last name

- Author's first initial and middle initial, if available

- Copyright year

- Title of paper or article abstract is from

- Journal title

- Volume number

- Page number(s)

To create this reference, follow these steps:

1. Indent one-half inch and type the author's last name in full, followed by a comma and a space.

2. Type the author's first initial (*not* the full first name), followed by a period and a space, then the middle initial (if available), followed by a period and a space. If the author's middle name is not listed, just use the first initial.

Remember: Never, never use the full first name!

3. Type the copyright year in parentheses, followed by a period and a space.

4. Type the title of the paper or article the abstract is from, followed by a period and a space. Use a capital letter on the first word, but use lower-case letters on all the other words unless they are proper nouns.

   NOTE: If the title of the journal or periodical itself does not include the word "abstracts," type "Abstract" in brackets between the last word of the title and the period, as shown in the second example in Figure 81.

5. Type the title of the journal, followed by a comma, a space, and the volume number. Underline them. Capitalize all words of the title.

6. Type a space, and then the page number and a period.

   NOTE: Notice that the "p." is not included in the page number shown in Figure 81. The "p." or "pp." is not used when the volume number is included.

7. If your reference continues to a second line, doublespace the second line and begin it back at the left margin.

Follow this format exactly. See Appendix F for a complete list of references.

```
        Smith, H. N. (1992).   Five prehistoric sites

in Orange County, California.   Abstracts of the Journal

of the Southwest Archeological Association, 18, 250.
```

```
        Smith, H. N. (1992).   Five prehistoric sites

in Orange County, California [Abstract].   Southwest

Archeological Association, 18, 250.
```

Figure 81. Examples of a Reference of an Abstract as an Original Source.

Referencing an Abstract From a Secondary Source

Sometimes, you will find an abstract that you want to reference that is referenced in someone else's work. A reference for an abstract from a secondary source is shown in Figure 82 and consists of the following elements:

- Author's last name

- Author's first initial and middle initial, if available

- Copyright year

- Title of paper or article abstract is from

- Journal title

- Volume number

- Page number(s)

- Secondary source information

To create this reference, follow these steps:

1. Indent one-half inch and type the author's last name in full, followed by a comma and a space.

2. Type the author's first initial (*not* the full first name), followed by a period and a space, then the middle initial (if available), followed by a period and a space. If the author's middle name is not listed, just use the first initial.

Remember: Never, never use the full first name!

3. Type the copyright year of the *original* abstract in parentheses, followed by a period and a space.

4. Type the title of the paper or article the abstract is from, followed by a period and a space. Use a capital letter on the first word, but use lower-case letters on all the other words unless they are proper nouns.

    NOTE: If the title of the journal or periodical itself does not include the word "abstracts," type "Abstract" in brackets between the last word of the title and the period, as shown in Figure 82.

5. Type the title of the journal, followed by a comma, a space, the volume number, and another comma. Underline all of these. Capitalize all words of the title.

6. Type a space, and then the page number, a period, and a space.

    NOTE: Notice that the "p." is not included in the page number shown in Figure 82. The "p." or "pp." is not used when the volume number is included.

7. Cite the secondary source information, including the source and title of the book or periodical (underlined and separated by a colon; the copyright date; the volume number, if available (underlined); and the abstract number, if available.

8. If your reference continues to a second line, doublespace the second line and begin it back at the left margin.

9. If you are using only the abstract and not the entire article as the source, reference the collection of abstracts in parentheses.

    NOTE: If the date of the secondary source is different from the date of the original source, include both dates in the your text citation (in the body of your paper). Cite the original source date first, type a slash, then type the secondary source date (e.g., (1992/1993)).

Follow this format exactly. See Appendix F for a complete list of references.

Smith, H. N. (1992). Five prehistoric sites in

Orange County, California [Abstract]. <u>Journal of the</u>

<u>Southwest Archeological Association, 18,</u> 12-19. (From

<u>ArcSCAN: The american southwest monthly,</u> 1994, <u>7,</u>

Abstract No. 151) (Abstracts of the Journal of the

Southwest Archaeological Association)

Figure 82. Example of a Reference of an Abstract as a Secondary Source.

Referencing a Periodical Published Annually

A reference for a periodical published annually is shown in Figure 83 and consists of the following elements:

- Author's last name

- Author's first initial and middle initial, if available

- Copyright year

- Title of paper or article abstract is from

- Journal title

- Volume number

- Page number(s)

To create this reference, follow these steps:

1. Indent one-half inch and type the author's last name in full, followed by a comma.

2. Type the author's first initial (*not* the full first name), followed by a period and a space, then the middle initial (if available), followed by a period, a comma, and a space. If the author's middle name is not listed, just use the first initial.

Remember: Never, never use the full first name!

3. Type the copyright year of the original abstract in parentheses, followed by a period and a space.

4. Type the title of the paper or article, followed by a period and a space. Use a capital letter on the first word, but use lower-case letters on all the other words unless they are proper nouns.

5. Type the title of the journal, followed by a comma, a space, the volume number, and another comma. Underline them. Capitalize all words of the title.

6. Type a space, and then the page number(s) and a period.

NOTE: Notice that the "p." is not included in the page number shown in Figure 83. The "p." or "pp." is not used when the volume number is included.

7. If your reference continues to a second line, doublespace the second line and begin it back at the left margin.

Follow this format exactly. See Appendix F for a complete list of references.

    Smith, H. N. (1992).   Trends in human resources.

Annual Review of Business, 18, 12-19.

Figure 83. Example of a Reference of a Periodical Published Annually.

Referencing a Work Discussed in a Secondary Source

Sometimes you will want to reference an article or book that is cited in someone else's work. In the List of References, list the information of the secondary source. Follow the rules for the type of reference it is; i.e., a book, journal article, newspaper article, etc.

Referencing Books

This section shows you how to reference a book with:

- one author

- two authors

- multiple authors

- a group author

- an editor

- an author and editor

- no author or editor

- a subtitle

- an article or chapter in a book

- an article or chapter in an edited book

When you reference books, you must include the city where the publisher is located. If the city does not appear in Table 15, you must include the two-letter state or territory code (see Table 13, page 56) or the country name.

Table 15. Cities not Needing State or Territory Code or Country Name in the Reference List.

AMERICAN CITIES		FOREIGN CITIES	
Baltimore	New York	Amsterdam	Paris
Boston	Philadelphia	Jerusalem	Rome
Chicago	San Francisco	London	Stockholm
Los Angeles		Milan	Tokyo
		Moscow	Vienna

Referencing a Book With One Author

A reference for a book with one author appears as shown in Figure 84, and consists of the following elements:

- Author's last name

- Author's first initial and middle initial, if available

- Year book was copyrighted

- Title of book

- City where publisher is located

- Name of publisher

To create this reference, follow these steps:

1. Indent one-half inch and type the author's last name in full, followed by a comma and a space.

2. Type the author's first initial (*not* the full first name), followed by a period and a space, then the middle initial (if available), followed by a period and a space. If the author's middle name is not listed, just use the first initial.

Remember: Never, never use the full first name!

3. Then type the copyright year in parentheses, followed by a period and a space.

4. Type the book title and underline it. Only the first word has a capital letter; the rest of the words are lower case.

   Place a period after the title, then a space.

5. Then type the city of publication, a colon, a space, then the name of the publisher, followed by a period. Include the two-letter state code or country name if the city is not listed in Table 15 on page 161 (i.e., Blue Ridge Summit, PA). For the state code abbreviation, see Table 13, page 56.

6. If your reference continues to a second line, doublespace the second line and begin it at the left margin.

Follow this format exactly. See Appendix F for a complete list of references.

    Parris, C. A. (1969). <u>Mastering executive arts and</u>

<u>skills</u>. New York: Atheneum.

Figure 84.   Example of a Reference of a Book with One Author.

Referencing a Book With Two Authors

A reference for a book with two authors appears as shown in Figure 85 and consists of the following elements:

- Both authors' last names

- Both authors' first initials and middle initials, if available

- Year book was copyrighted

- Title of book

- City where publisher is located

- Name of publisher

To create this reference, follow these steps:

1. Indent one-half inch and type the first author's last name in full, followed by a comma and a space.

2. Type the first author's first initial (*not* the full first name), followed by a period and a space, then the middle initial (if available), followed by a period, a comma, and a space. If the author's middle name is not listed, just use the first initial.

Remember: Never, never use the full first name!

3. Type in an ampersand (&) and a space.

4. Type the second author's last name, followed by a comma and a space.

5. Type the second author's first initial (*not* the full first name!), followed by a period and a space, then the middle initial (if available), followed by a period and a space. If the author's middle name is not listed, just use the first initial.

6. Then put the copyright year in parentheses, followed by a period and a space.

7. Type the book title and underline it. Only the first word has a capital letter; the rest of the words are lower case.

   Place a period after the title, then a space.

8. Then type the city of publication, a colon, a space, then the name of the publisher, followed by a period. Include the two-letter state code or country name if the city is not listed in Table 15 on page 161 (i.e., Blue Ridge Summit, PA). For the state code abbreviation, see Table 13, page 56.

9. If your reference continues to a second line, doublespace the second line and begin it back at the left margin.

Follow this format exactly. See Appendix F for a complete list of references.

```
Spetch, M. L., & Wilkie, D. M. (1983).  How to

bullet-proof your manuscript.  New York: Atheneum.
```

Figure 85. Example of a Reference of a Book With Two Authors.

Referencing a Book With Multiple Authors

A reference for a book with multiple (three or more) authors appears as shown in Figure 86 and consists of the following elements:

- Authors' last names

- Authors' first initials and middle initials, if available

- Year book was copyrighted

- Title of book

- City where publisher is located

- Name of publisher

To create this reference, follow these steps:

1. Indent one-half inch and type the first author's last name in full, followed by a comma and a space.

2. Type the first author's first initial (*not* the full first name), followed by a period and a space, then the middle initial, if available, followed by a period, a comma, and a space. If the author's middle name is not listed, just use the first initial.

Remember: Never, never use the full first name!

3. Type the second author's last name, followed by a comma and a space.

4. Type the second author's first initial (*not* the full first name!), followed by a period and a space, then the middle initial, if available, followed by a period and a space. If the author's middle name is not listed, just use the first initial.

5. Repeat Steps 3 and 4 for all authors except the last.

6. Type in an ampersand (&) and a space.

7. Type the last author's last name, followed by a comma and a space.

8. Type the last author's first initial (*not* the full first name!), followed by a period and a space, then the middle initial, if available, followed by a period and a space. If the author's middle name is not listed, just use the first initial.

9. Type the copyright year in parentheses, followed by a period.

10. Type the book title and underline it. Only the first word has a capital letter; the rest of the words are lower case.

    Place a period after the title, then a space.

11. Type the city of publication, a colon, a space, then the name of the publisher, followed by a period.   Include the two-letter state code or country name if the city is not listed in Table 15 on page 161 (i.e., Blue Ridge Summit, PA). For the state code abbreviation, see Table 13, page 56.

12. If your reference continues to a second line, doublespace the second line and begin it back at the left margin.

Follow this format exactly. See Appendix F for a complete list of references.

```
     Sanders, T. J., Jones, L., Lyle, B. R., & Brown,

K. G. (1992).  Effective leadership in the 90s.  New

York: Management Press.
```

Figure 86. Example of a Reference of a Book With Multiple Authors.

Referencing a Book With a Group Author (Company or Agency)

Some books are published with a company or government agency listed as the author. The American Management Association may publish a book, for instance, and list no author or editor other than itself.

A reference for a book with a group author is different from a reference of a book with an author. It appears as shown in Figure 87 and consists of the following elements:

- Name of publisher

- Year book was copyrighted

- Title of book

- City where publisher is located

To create this reference, follow these steps:

1. Indent one-half inch and type the publisher's name (used in lieu of an author's name), followed by a period and a space.

2. Type the copyright year in parentheses, followed by a period and a space.

3. Type the book title, then underline it. Only the first word has a capital letter; the rest of the words are lower case.

   Place a period after the title, then a space.

4. Type the city of publication, followed by a colon. Include the two-letter state code or country name if the city is not listed in Table 15 on page 161 (i.e., Blue Ridge Summit, PA). For the state code abbreviation, see Table 13, page 56.

5. Type the word "Author," and begin it with a capital "A." This represents the publisher.

6. If your reference continues to a second line, doublespace the second line and begin it back at the left margin.

Follow this format exactly.   See Appendix F for a complete list of references.

```
      American Management Association (1992). PCs today.

New York: Author.
```

Figure 87. Example of Reference of a Book With a Group Author.

Referencing a Book With an Editor

Many times, books are edited rather than authored; that is, they are a collection of articles or stories by other people, and the final book is put together by another person altogether. The cover and title page of the book will tell you that the person is the editor rather than the writer.

A reference for a book with an editor appears as shown in Figure 88 and consists of the following elements:

- Editor's last name

- Editor's first initial and middle initial, if available

- The abbreviation "Ed."

- Year book was copyrighted

- Title of book

- City where publisher is located

- Name of publisher

To create this reference, follow these steps:

1. Indent one-half inch and type the editor's last name in full, followed by a comma and a space.

2. Type the editor's first initial (*not* the full first name), followed by a period and a space, then the middle initial (if available), followed by a period, a comma, and a space. If the editor's middle name is not listed, just use the first initial.

Remember: Never, never use the full first name!

3. Type "Ed" in parentheses, followed by a period and a space.

4. Type the copyright year in parentheses, followed by a period and a space.

5. Type the book title, then underline it. Only the first word has a capital letter; the rest are lower case. Follow the title with a period and a space.

6. Type the city of publication, a colon, a space, then the name of the publisher, followed by a period. Include the two-letter state code or country name if the city is not listed in Table 15 on page 161 (i.e., Blue Ridge Summit, PA). For the state code abbreviation, see Table 13, page 56.

7. If your reference continues to a second line, doublespace the second line and begin it back at the left margin.

Follow this format exactly. See Appendix F for a complete list of references.

```
    Jones, J. (Ed.). (1992). PCs today. New York:

Doubleday.
```

Figure 88. Example of a Reference of a Book With an Editor.

Referencing a Book With an Author and an Editor

A reference for a book with an author and an editor appears as shown in Figure 89 and consists of the following elements:

- Author's last name

- Author's first initial, and middle initial, if available

- Year book was copyrighted

- Title of book

- Editor's first initial, and middle initial, if available

- Editor's last name

- City where publisher is located

- Name of publisher

To create this reference, follow these steps:

1. Indent one-half inch and type the author's last name in full, followed by a comma and a space.

2. Type the author's first initial (*not* the full first name), followed by a period and a space, then the middle initial (if available), followed by a period and a space. If the author's middle name is not listed, just use the first initial.

Remember: Never, never use the full first name!

3. Type the copyright year in parentheses, followed by a period and a space.

4. Type the book title and underline it. Only the first word has a capital letter; the rest of the words are lower case.

5. In parentheses, type the editor's first initial, a period and a space, and the middle initial (if available), followed by a period and a space. Then type the editor's last name, followed by a comma, a space, and the abbreviation "Ed.," followed by a period, the second parenthesis, and another period. Make sure the "E" is capitalized.

6. Type the city of publication, a colon, a space, then the name of the publisher, followed by a period. Include the two-letter state code or country name if the city is not listed in Table 15 on page 161 (i.e., Blue Ridge Summit, PA). For the state code abbreviation, see Table 13, page 56.

7. If your reference continues to a second line, doublespace the second line and begin it back at the left margin.

Follow this format exactly. See Appendix F for a complete list of references.

Harrison, P. R. (1989). The manager's world (F. G.

Taylor, Ed.). Los Angeles: Business Press.

Figure 89. Example of a Book Reference with an Author and an Editor.

Referencing a Book With No Author or Editor

Many books do not list an author or editor at all, just the title. Most reference books fall in this category.

A reference for a book with no author is different from a reference of a book with an author. It appears as shown in Figure 90 and consists of the following elements:

- Title of book

- Edition, if relevant

- Year book was copyrighted

- City where publisher is located

- Publisher's name

To create this reference, follow these steps:

1. Indent one-half inch and type the book title, then underline it and add a space after the last word. Only the first word has a capital letter; the rest are lower case.

   There is one exception: If the title contains a proper name, capitalize all words in that proper name.

2. In parentheses, type the edition number and the abbreviation "ed" followed by a period. Add another period after the second parenthesis.

3. Type the copyright year in parentheses, followed by a period and a space.

4. Then type the city of publication, followed by a colon. Include the two-letter state or country name if the city is not listed in Table 15 on page 161 (i.e., Blue Ridge Summit, PA). For the state code abbreviation, see Table 13, page 56.

5. Type the publisher's name, followed by a period.

6. If your reference continues to a second line, doublespace the second line and begin it back at the left margin.

Follow this format exactly. See Appendix F for a complete list of references.

```
     The student's dictionary (4th ed.). (1992).

New York: Wallace.
```

Figure 90. Example of Book Reference With No Author or Editor.

Referencing a Book With a Subtitle

What if the book has a subtitle?

A reference for a book with a subtitle appears as shown in Figure 91 and consists of the following elements:

- Author's last name

- Author's first initial and middle initial, if available

- Year book was copyrighted

- Title of book

- City where publisher is located

- Name of publisher

To create this reference, follow these steps:

1. Indent one-half inch and type the author's last name in full, followed by a comma and a space.

   NOTE: If this book has two authors, multiple authors, or no author, see the pages showing how to reference those forms (pp. 164-167, 174-175).

2. Type the author's first initial (*not* the full first name), followed by a period and a space, then the middle initial (if available), followed by a period and a space. If the author's middle name is not listed, just use the first initial.

Remember: Never, never use the full first name!

3. Then type the copyright year in parentheses, followed by a period.

4a. Type the title of the book, followed by a colon. Only the first word has a capital letter; the rest of the words are lower case.

 b. Then type the subtitle, beginning once again with a capital letter. The remaining words are lowercase.

4. Cont'd.

   c. Underline the entire title.

   d. Place a period after the title, then a space.

5. Then type the city of publication, a colon, a space, then the name of the publisher, followed by a period.   Include the two-letter state or country name if the city is not listed in Table 15 on page 161 (i.e., Blue Ridge Summit, PA). For the state code abbreviation, see Table 13, page 56.

6. If your reference continues to a second line, doublespace the second line and begin it back at the left margin.

Follow this format exactly. See Appendix F for a complete list of references.

```
Bernstein, T. M. (1965).  The careful writer: A

modern guide to English usage.  New York: Atheneum.
```

Figure 91.   Example of a Book Reference With a Subtitle.

Referencing an Article or Chapter in a Book

You can also reference an article or chapter within a book if the author's name appears on it.

A reference for an article or chapter within a book appears as shown in Figure 92 and consists of the following elements:

- Author's last name

- Author's first initial and middle initial, if available

- Year book was copyrighted

- Title of article or chapter

- Name of book

- Page numbers of article or chapter

- City where publisher is located

- Name of publisher

To create this reference, follow these steps:

1. Indent one-half inch and type the author's last name in full, followed by a comma and a space.

2. Type the author's first initial (*not* the full first name), followed by a period and a space, then the middle initial (if available), followed by a period, a comma, and a space. If the author's middle name is not listed, just use the first initial.

Remember: Never, never use the full first name!

3. Type the copyright year in parentheses, followed by a period.

4. Type the title of the article. Use a capital letter on the first word, but use lower-case letters on all the other words. End the title with a period.

5. Type the word "In" in plain type, followed by the book title. Only the first word of the title has a capital letter; the rest of the words are lower case, unless one is a proper name. Underline the title.

6. Type the page numbers in parentheses. Be sure to use "pp," followed by a period, if there is a range of pages. End with another period.

7. Type the city of publication, a colon, a space, then the name of the publisher, followed by a period.   Include the two-letter state code or country name if the city is not listed in Table 15 on page 161 (i.e., Blue Ridge Summit, PA). For the state code abbreviation, see Table 13, page 56.

8. If your reference continues to a second line, doublespace the second line and begin it back at the left margin.

Follow this format exactly. See Appendix F for a complete list of references.

```
    Jones, J. T. (1992). The workplace in the year

2000. In PCs today (pp. 113-120).  New York: Doubleday.
```

Figure 92. Example of a Reference of an Article or Chapter in a Book.

Referencing an Article or Chapter in an Edited Book

You can also reference an article or chapter within an edited book if the author's name appears on it.

A reference for an article or chapter within an edited book appears as shown in Figure 93 and consists of the following elements:

- Author's last name

- Author's first initial and middle initial, if available

- Year book was copyrighted

- Title of article or chapter

- Editor's first initial and middle initial, if available

- Editor's last name

- Name of book

- Page numbers of article or chapter

- City where publisher is located

- Name of publisher

To create this reference, follow these steps:

1. Indent one-half inch and type the author's last name in full, followed by a comma and a space.

2. Type the author's first initial (*not* the full first name), followed by a period and a space, then the middle initial (if available), followed by a period, a comma, and a space. If the author's middle name is not listed, just use the first initial.

Remember: Never, never use the full first name!

3. Type the copyright year in parentheses, followed by a period.

4. Type the title of the article. Use a capital letter on the first word, but use lower-case letters on all the other words. End the title with a period.

5. Type the word "In" in plain type, followed by the editor's first initial, a space, and the editor's middle initial, if available, and a space.

6. In parentheses, type "Ed," followed by a period. After the closing parenthesis, type a comma and a space.

7. Type the book title and underline it. Only the first word of the title has a capital letter; the rest are lower case, unless one is a proper name.

8. Type the page numbers in parentheses. Be sure to use "pp," followed by a period, if there is a range of pages. End with another period.

9. Type the city of publication, a colon, a space, then the name of the publisher, followed by a period. Include the two-letter state code or country name if the city is not listed in Table 15 on page 161 (i.e., Blue Ridge Summit, PA). For the state code abbreviation, see Table 13, page 56.

10. If your reference continues to a second line, doublespace the second line and begin it back at the left margin.

Follow this format exactly. See Appendix F for a complete list of references.

```
     Jones, J. T. (1992). The workplace in the year

2000. In S. L. Graves (Ed.), PCs today (pp. 201-210).

New York: Acme Press.
```

Figure 93. Example of a Reference of an Article or Chapter in an Edited Book.

Referencing a Company Brochure

Most company brochures have no authors. A reference for a brochure appears as shown in Figure 94 and consists of the following elements:

- Name of company whose name appears on the brochure

- Year of publication, if available

- Title of brochure

- Number of edition, if applicable

- The word "Brochure"

- City and state where brochure was published

- The word "Author"

To create this reference, follow these steps:

1. Indent one-half inch and type the company name, followed by a period and a space. Capitalize the first letter of all the words in the name.

2. Type the copyright year, if available, in parentheses, followed by a period and a space.

3. Type the title of the brochure and underline it. Use a capital letter on the first word, but use lower-case letters on all the other words. Press the space bar.

4. If there is an edition number, type it in parentheses and press the space bar.

5. Type the word "Brochure" in brackets, followed by a period and a space. Capitalize the "B."

6. Type the city of publication, if available, followed by a colon and a space. Include the two-letter state code if the city is other than New York, Chicago, Los Angeles, or San Francisco.

7. Type the word "Author," followed by a period. Capitalize the "A."

8. If your reference continues to a second line, doublespace the second line and begin it back at the left margin.

Follow this format exactly. See Appendix F for a complete list of references.

```
Stanley Equipment Co. (1994).  Ergonomic furniture

for health and safety (2nd ed.) [Brochure].  New York:

Author.
```

Figure 94. Example of a Reference of a Company Brochure.

Referencing Encyclopedias and Dictionaries

You can reference encyclopedias or dictionaries in four ways:

- With an author

- Without an author

- With an editor

- As an article in an encyclopedia

Referencing an Encyclopedia Set or Dictionary With an Author

A reference for an encyclopedia set or dictionary with an author appears as shown in Figure 95 and consists of the following elements:

- Author's last name

- Author's first and middle initials, if available

- Year encyclopedia set or dictionary was copyrighted

- Title of encyclopedia set or dictionary

- Number of edition, if relevant

- Volumes numbers, if encyclopedia set

- City where publisher is located

- Name of publisher

To create this reference, follow these steps:

1. Indent one-half inch and type the author's last name in full, followed by a comma and a space.

2. Type the author's first initial (*not* the full first name), followed by a period and a space, then the middle initial (if available), followed by a period and a space.

Remember: Never, never use the full first name!

3. Type the copyright year in parentheses, followed by a period and a space.

4. Type the encyclopedia set or dictionary title and underline it. Only the first word has a capital letter; the rest of the words are lower case. Follow the title with a period and a space.

5. Place the edition number in parentheses. Abbreviate the word "edition" as "ed" (use lower-case letters), followed by a period. If there are no volume numbers to reference, go to Step 5a. If there are, go to Step 5b.

   a. Close the parentheses and place a period and a space right after the second parenthesis. Go to Step 6.

   b. Type a comma and a space. Then type the word "Volume(s)" as the abbreviated form "Vol(s)" and follow it with a period and a space. Add the volume numbers, close the parentheses, then type a period and a space.

6. Type the city of publication, a colon, a space, then the name of the publisher, followed by a period.   Include the two-letter state code if the city is not listed in Table 15 on page 161.

7. If your reference continues to a second line, doublespace the second line and begin it back at the left margin.

Follow this format exactly. See Appendix F for a complete list of references.

```
   Smith, R. F. (1994). Encyclopedia of ecology.

(3rd ed., Vols. 1-10). New York: Acme.
```

```
   Jones, T. M. (1992). Dictionary of computer terms.

(2nd ed.). New York: Times Books.
```

Figure 95. Examples of References From an Encyclopedia Set and Dictionary With an Author.

Referencing an Encyclopedia Set or Dictionary With No Author

A reference for an encyclopedia set or dictionary with no author appears as shown in Figure 96 and consists of the following elements:

- Publisher's name

- Year encyclopedia set or dictionary was copyrighted

- Title of encyclopedia set or dictionary

- Number of edition, if relevant

- Volumes numbers, if encyclopedia set

- City where publisher is located

To create this reference, follow these steps:

1. Indent one-half inch and type the publisher's name in full, followed by a period and a space.

2. Type the copyright year in parentheses, followed by a period and a space.

3. Type the encyclopedia set or dictionary title and underline it. Only the first word has a capital letter; the rest of the words are lower case.

   Place a period after the title, then a space.

6. Place the edition number in parentheses. Abbreviate the word "edition" as "ed." (use lower-case letters), followed by a period. If there are no volume numbers to reference, go to Step 6a. If there are volume numbers to reference, go to Step 6b.

   a. Close the parentheses and place a period and a space right after the second parenthesis. Go to Step 7.

b. Type a comma and a space. Then type the word "Volume(s)" as the abbreviated form "Vol(s)" and follow it with a period and a space. Type the volume numbers, close the parenthesis, then type a period and a space.

7. Then type the city of publication, followed by a period. Include the two-letter state code if the city is not listed in Table 15 on page 161.

8. If your reference continues to a second line, doublespace the second line and begin it back at the left margin.

Follow this format exactly. See Appendix F for a complete list of references.

```
     Acme. (1994). Encyclopedia of ecology. (3rd ed.,

Vols. 1-10). New York.
```

```
     Times Books. (1992). Dictionary of business

terms. (2nd ed.). New York.
```

Figure 96. Examples of References From an Encyclopedia Set and Dictionary With No Author.

Referencing an Encyclopedia Set or Dictionary With an Editor

A reference for an encyclopedia set or dictionary with an editor appears as shown in Figure 97 and consists of the following elements:

- Editor's last name

- Editor's first and middle initials, if available

- Year encyclopedia set or dictionary was copyrighted

- Title of encyclopedia set or dictionary

- Number of edition, if relevant

- Volumes numbers, if encyclopedia set

- City where publisher is located

- Name of publisher

To create this reference, follow these steps:

1. Indent one-half inch and type the editor's last name in full, followed by a comma and a space.

2. Type the editor's first initial (*not* the full first name), followed by a period and a space, then the middle initial (if available), followed by a period and a space. If the editor's middle name is not listed, just use the first initial.

Remember: Never, never use the full first name!

3. Type the letters "Ed," followed by a period, within parentheses. Follow that with another period and a space.

4. Type the copyright year in parentheses, followed by a period and a space.

5. Type the encyclopedia set or dictionary title and underline it. Only the first word has a capital letter; the rest of the words are lower case. Place a period after the title, then a space.

6. Place the edition number in parentheses. Abbreviate the word "edition" as "ed" (use lower-case letters), followed by a period. If there are no volume numbers to reference, go to Step 6a. If there are volume numbers to reference, go to Step 6b.

    a. Close the parentheses and place a period right after the second parenthesis. Go to Step 7.

    b. Type the word "Volume(s)" as the abbreviated form "Vol(s)" and follow it with a period and a space. Type the volume numbers, close the parentheses, then type a period and a space.

7. Then type the city of publication, a colon, a space, then the name of the publisher, followed by a period. Include the two-letter state code if the city is other not listed in Table 15 on page 161.

8. If your reference continues to a second line, doublespace the second line and begin it back at the left margin.

Follow this format exactly. See Appendix F for a complete list of references.

Smith, R. F. (Ed.). (1994). Encyclopedia of

ecology. (3rd ed., Vols. 1-10). New York: Acme.

Jones, T. M. (Ed.). (1992). Dictionary of

business terms. (2nd ed.). New York: Times

Books.

Figure 97. Examples of References From an Encyclopedia Set and Dictionary With an Editor.

Referencing an Article in an Encyclopedia

Articles in encyclopedias may or may not have an author. The following sections show you how to reference both types.

Referencing an Article in an Encyclopedia With an Author

A reference for an article in an encyclopedia or encyclopedia set appears as shown in Figure 98 and consists of the following elements:

- Author's last name

- Author's first initial, and middle initial, if available

- Year encyclopedia or set was copyrighted

- Title of article

- Title of encyclopedia or set

- Number of edition, if relevant

- Volume number, if encyclopedia set

- City where publisher is located

- Name of publisher

To create this reference, follow these steps:

1. Indent one-half inch and type the author's last name in full, followed by a comma and a space.

2. Type the author's first initial (*not* the full first name), followed by a period and a space, then the middle initial (if available), followed by a period and a space. If the author's middle name is not listed, just use the first initial.

Remember: Never, never use the full first name!

3. Type the copyright year in parentheses, followed by a period and a space.

4. Type the title of the article in plain type. Use a capital letter on the first word, but use lower-case letters on the remaining words. End the title with a period and a space.

5. Type the word "In" in plain type, using a capital "I." Then type the title of the encyclopedia or set and underline it. Only the first word has a capital letter; the rest of the words are lower case. Follow the title with a period and a space.

6. If there is a volume number to reference, continue with this step. If not, go to Step 7.

   Place the volume number in parentheses. Abbreviate the word "Volume" as "Vol," followed by a period and a space, then type the volume number, followed by a comma and a space. Type the letter "p," followed by a period and a space (or "pp.," if there is a range of pages). Then type the page number(s), followed by the second parenthesis, a period, and a space. Go to Step 8.

7. Type an opening parenthesis, then the letter "P," followed by a period (or "Pp.," if there is a range of pages). Then type the page number(s), followed by the second parenthesis, a period, and a space.

8. Type the city of publication, a colon, a space, then the name of the publisher, followed by a period. Include the two-letter state code if the city is not listed in Table 15 on page 161.

9. If your reference continues to a second line, doublespace the second line and begin it back at the left margin.

Follow this format exactly. See Appendix F for a complete list of references.

```
Jamison, L. R. (1991). The disappearing ozone

layer. In Encyclopedia of ecology. (Vol. 4, pp. 22-

27). New York: Acme.
```

Figure 98. Example of a Reference of an Article in an Encyclopedia With an Author.

Referencing an Article With No Author in an Encyclopedia

A reference for an article with no author in an encyclopedia appears as shown in Figure 99 and consists of the following elements:

- Title of article

- Year encyclopedia was copyrighted

- Title of encyclopedia

- Number of edition, if relevant

- Volume number, if encyclopedia set

- City where publisher is located

- Name of publisher

To create this reference, follow these steps:

1. Indent one-half inch and type the title of the article in plain type. Use a capital letter on the first word, but use lower-case letters on the remaining words. End the title with a period and a space.

2. Type the copyright year in parentheses, followed by a period and a space.

3. Type the word "In" in plain type, using a capital "I." Then type the title of the encyclopedia or set and underline it. Only the first word has a capital letter; the rest of the words are lower case. Follow the title with a period and a space.

4. If there is a volume number to reference, continue with this step. If not, go to Step 5.

   Place the volume number in parentheses. Abbreviate the word "Volume" as "Vol," followed by a period and a space, then type the volume number, followed by a comma and a space. Type the letter "p," followed by a period (or "pp.," if there is a range of pages). Then type the page number(s), followed by the second parenthesis and a period. Go to Step 6.

5. Type an opening parenthesis, then the letter "p," followed by a period (or "pp.," if there is a range of pages). Then type the page number(s), followed by the second parenthesis and a period and a space.

6. Type the city of publication, a colon, a space, then the name of the publisher, followed by a period. Include the two-letter state code if the city is not listed in Table 15 on page 161.

7. If your reference continues to a second line, doublespace the second line and begin it back at the left margin.

Follow this format exactly. See Appendix F for a complete list of references.

```
The disappearing ozone layer. (1994). In Encyclo-

pedia of ecology. (Vol. 4, pp. 22-27). New York: Acme.
```

Figure 99. Example of a Reference of an Article With No Author in an Encyclopedia.

Referencing Government Publications

This section shows you how to reference a report from the:

- Government Printing Office (GPO)

- National Technical Information Service (NTIS)

Referencing a Report From the Government Printing Office (GPO)

The Government Printing Office (GPO) prints all the publications from federal agencies. Many are available free or at a low-cost, and you may find these helpful in your research. A reference of a GPO publication appears in Figure 100 and consists of the following elements:

- Issuing agency's name

- Year report was copyrighted

- Title of report

- Number of report, if relevant

- Washington, DC

- U.S. Government Printing Office

To create this reference, follow these steps:

1. Indent one-half inch and type the issuing agency's name in full, followed by a period and a space.

2. Type the copyright year in parentheses, followed by a period and a space. (Include the month, if relevant.)

3. Type the report title and underline it. Only the first word has a capital letter; the rest of the words are lower case.

4. Place the publication number in parentheses. Abbreviate the word "number" as "No," followed by a period. After the closing parenthesis, type a period and a space.

5. Type "Washington, DC," followed by a colon, a space, and "U.S. Government Printing Office," followed by a period.

6. If your reference continues to a second line, doublespace the second line and begin it back at the left margin.

Follow this format exactly. See Appendix F for a complete list of references.

Small Business Administration. (1976). <u>Checklist</u>

<u>for going into business</u>. (Small Marketers Aid No. 71).

Washington, DC: U.S. Government Printing Office.

Figure 100. Example of a Reference of a Report From the GPO.

Referencing a Report From the National Technical Information Service (NTIS)

A reference of a National Technical Information Service (NTIS) publication appears in Figure 101 and consists of the following elements:

- Author's name(s)

- Year report was copyrighted

- Title of report

- Number of report, if relevant

- City of publication

- Publisher's name

To create this reference, follow these steps:

1. Indent one-half inch and type the author's last name in full, followed by a comma and a space.

2. Type the author's first initial (*not* the full first name), followed by a period and a space, then the middle initial (if available), followed by a period and a space. If the author's middle name is not listed, just use the first initial.

Remember: Never, never use the full first name!

3. Type the copyright year in parentheses, followed by a period and a space.

4. Type the report title and underline it. Only the first word has a capital letter; the rest of the words are lower case. End with a period and a space.

5. Type the city of publication, followed by the state code, if the city is not listed in Table 15 on page 161, then a colon and a space.

6. Type the publisher's name, followed by a period and a space.

7. Place the publication number in parentheses. Abbreviate the word "number" as "No," followed by a period; however, do *not* place a period after the second parenthesis.

8. If your reference continues to a second line, doublespace the second line and begin it back at the left margin.

Follow this format exactly. See Appendix F for a complete list of references.

```
    Jones, J. T. (1993).   Covariation of infant health

problems. Elm City, NV: University of the West. (NTIS

No. AA 10-444 300/AS)
```

Figure 101. Example of a Report From the National Technical Information Service (NTIS).

Referencing Academic Material

This section shows you how to reference:

- a report from a university

- a report from a private organization

- proceedings

- an unpublished paper presented at a meeting

- doctoral dissertations and master's theses

Referencing a Report From a University

A reference of a report from a university appears in Figure 102 and consists of the following elements:

- Author's name(s)

- Year report was copyrighted

- Title of report

- Number of report, if relevant

- City where the university is located

- University's name

- Name of the department issuing the report

To create this reference, follow these steps:

1. Indent one-half inch and type the author's last name in full, followed by a comma and a space.

2. Type the author's first initial (*not* the full first name), followed by a period, a space, then the middle initial (if available), then another period and a space. If the author's middle name is not listed, just use the first initial.

Remember: Never, never use the full first name!

3. Type the copyright year in parentheses, followed by a period and a space.

4a. Type the report title and underline it. Only the first word has a capital letter; the rest of the words are lower case. Follow the title with a space.

  b. Place the publication number in parentheses. Abbreviate any words associated with it.; abbreviate the word "number" as "No," followed by a period and a space.

  c. After the closing parenthesis, type a period and a space.

5. Type the city of publication, followed by a comma, a space, then the two-letter state code (or country name, if this is a foreign publication), a colon, and a space. (If the state is included in the university's name, you don't need to repeat the state name here.)

6. Type the name of the university, followed by a comma and a space.

7. Type the name of the department issuing the report. End with a period.

8. If your reference continues to a second line, doublespace the second line and begin it back at the left margin.

Follow this format exactly. See Appendix F for a complete list of references.

Jones, J. T. (1993). Changes in management philo-

sophy from 1980 to 1990 (Tech. Rep. No. 6). Main City,

IA: Eastern State University, School of Business.

Figure 102. Example of a Reference of a Report From a University.

Referencing a Report From a Private Organization

Private organizations are institutes, foundations, etc. A reference of a report from a private organization appears in Figure 103 and consists of the following elements:

- Organization's name

- Year report was copyrighted (and month, if applicable)

- Title of report

- Number of report, if relevant

- City where the organization is located

- The word "Author"

To create this reference, follow these steps:

1. Indent one-half inch and type the organization's name in full, followed by a period and a space.

3. Type the copyright year in parentheses. Include the month, if available, as shown in Figure 103. Then type a period and a space.

4a. Type the report title and underline it. Only the first word has a capital letter; the rest of the words are lower case.

   b. Place the publication number, if available, in parentheses. Abbreviate the word "number" as "No," followed by a period and a space.

5. Type the city of publication, followed by a comma, a space, then the state two-letter code (or country name, if this is a foreign publication), a colon and a space.

6. Type the word "Author" and a period.

7. If your reference continues to a second line, doublespace the second line and begin it back at the left margin.

Follow this format exactly. See Appendix F for a complete list of references.

```
Acme Manufacturing, Inc. (1993, December).

Changes in management philosophy from 1980 to 1990

(Issue No. 6).  Main City, IA: Author.
```

Figure 103. Example of a Reference of a Report From a Private Organization.

Referencing Doctoral Dissertations

This section shows you how to reference a(n):

- Published doctoral dissertation abstracted in Dissertation Abstracts International (DAI) and

  ✔ obtained from University Microfilm

  ✔ obtained from the University

- Unpublished doctoral dissertation

Referencing a Published Dissertation Abstracted in Dissertation Abstracts International (DAI) and Obtained From University Microfilm

Check Dissertation Abstracts International (DAI) to see what other students have done on your topic. University Microfilm keeps microfilm copies of all dissertations created in the United States. A reference of a published dissertation abstracted in DAI and obtained from University Microfilm appears in Figure 104 and consists of the following elements:

- Author's name(s)

- Year dissertation was copyrighted

- Title of dissertation

- The words "Dissertation Abstracts International"

- Volume number

- Page and series number

- University Microfilms number

To create this reference, follow these steps:

1. Indent one-half inch and type the author's last name in full, followed by a comma and a space.

2. Type the author's first initial (*not* the full first name), a period, a space, the middle initial (if available), then another period and a space. If the author's middle name is not listed, just use the first initial.

Remember: Never, never use the full first name!

3. Type the copyright year in parentheses, followed by a period and a space.

4. Type the dissertation title, followed by a period and a space. Only the first word has a capital letter; the rest of the words are lower case.

5. Type the words "Dissertation Abstracts International," a comma, and a space. Type the volume number. Underline all of this.

6. If the issue number is available, type it in parentheses, followed by a comma and a space. If not, just type the comma and the space.

7. Type the page number and the series number (A is for humanities; B is for sciences), followed by a period and a space.

8. Type the University Microfilms reference number in parentheses. Abbreviate the word "Number" as "No."

9. If your reference continues to a second line, doublespace the second line and begin it back at the left margin.

Follow this format exactly. See Appendix F for a complete list of references.

```
Jones, J. T. (1993). The effects of bottom-up

management techniques on clerical employees in five high-

tech companies.  Dissertation Abstracts International,

53(01), 236B. (University Microfilms No. AAD93-12345)
```

Figure 104. Example of a Reference of a Published Dissertation Abstracted in DAI and Obtained From University Microfilm.

Referencing a Dissertation Abstracted in Dissertation Abstracts International (DAI) and Obtained From the University

A reference of a published dissertation abstracted in DAI and obtained from the University appears in Figure 105 and consists of the following elements:

- Author's name(s)

- Year dissertation was copyrighted in DAI

- Title of dissertation

- The words "Doctoral Dissertation"

- The name of the university

- The year on the cover page of the disseration

- The words "Dissertation Abstracts International"

- Volume number

- Page number(s)

To create this reference, follow these steps:

1. Indent one-half inch and type the author's last name in full, followed by a comma and a space.

2. Type the author's first initial (*not* the full first name), a period, a space, the middle initial (if available), then another period and a space. If the author's middle name is not listed, just use the first initial.

Remember: Never, never use the full first name!

3. Type the DAI copyright year in parentheses, followed by a period and a space.

4. Type the dissertation title. Only the first word has a capital letter; the rest of the words are lower case.

5. Type the words "Doctoral dissertation" in parentheses, followed by a comma and a space.

6. Type the name of the university, followed by a comma and a space.

7. Type the year on the cover page of the dissertation, followed by the second parenthesis and a period.

8. Type the words "Dissertation Abstracts International," a comma, a space, the volume number, and a comma. Underline all of this.

9. Type a space, then the DAI page numbers.

10. If your reference continues to a second line, doublespace the second line and begin it back at the left margin.

Follow this format exactly. See Appendix F for a complete list of references.

Jones, J. T. (1993). The effects of bottom-up management techniques on clerical employees in five high-tech companies. (Doctoral dissertation, Eastern State University, 1993). Dissertation Abstracts International, 53, Z4023.

Figure 105. Example of a Reference of a Dissertation Abstracted in DAI and Obtained From the University.

Referencing an Unpublished Dissertation

You might get some material from a dissertation on which someone is currently working. A reference of a unpublished dissertation appears in Figure 106 and consists of the following elements:

- Author's name(s)

- Year in which the material was written

- Title of dissertation

- The words " Unpublished doctoral dissertation"

- The name of the university

- The city (and state, if not in the university name) where the university is located

To create this reference, follow these steps:

1. Indent one-half inch and type the author's last name in full, followed by a comma and a space.

2. Type the author's first initial (*not* the full first name), a period, a space, the middle initial (if available), then another period and a space. If the author's middle name is not listed, just use the first initial.

Remember: Never, never use the full first name!

3. Type the year in which the material was written in parentheses, followed by a period and a space.

4. Type the dissertation title and underline it. Only the first word has a capital letter; the rest of the words are lower case. End with a period and a space.

5. Type the words "Unpublished doctoral dissertation," followed by a comma and a space.

6. Type the name of the university, followed by a comma and a space.

7. Type the city where the university is located. Include the two-letter state code if the state is not in the university name. End with a period.

8. If your reference continues to a second line, doublespace the second line and begin it back at the left margin.

Follow this format exactly. See Appendix F for a complete list of references.

Jones, J. T. (1993). The effects of bottom-up management techniques on clerical employees in five high-tech companies. Unpublished doctoral dissertation, Eastern State University, Elm City, CT.

Figure 106. Example of a Reference of an Unpublished Dissertation.

Referencing a Master's Thesis

This section shows you how to reference a(n):

- Published master's thesis abstracted in Master's Abstracts International (MAI) and obtained from University Microfilm

- Published master's thesis abstracted in Master's Abstracts International (MAI) and obtained from the University

- Unpublished master's thesis

Referencing a Published Thesis Abstracted in Master's Abstracts International (MAI) and Obtained From University Microfilm

Check Master's Abstracts International (MAI) to see what other students have done on your topic. University Microfilm keeps microfilm copies of all theses created in the United States. A reference of a published thesis abstracted in MAI and obtained from University Microfilm appears in Figure 107 and consists of the following elements:

- Author's name(s)

- Year thesis was copyrighted

- Title of thesis

- The words "Master's Abstracts International"

- Volume number

- Page number

- University's name

- University Microfilm's number

To create this reference, follow these steps:

1. Indent one-half inch and type the author's last name in full, followed by a comma and a space.

2. Type the author's first initial (*not* the full first name), a period, a space, the middle initial (if available), then another period and a space. If the author's middle name is not listed, just use the first initial.

Remember: Never, never use the full first name!

3. Type the copyright year in parentheses, followed by a period and a space.

4. Type the thesis title, followed by a period and a space. Only the first word has a capital letter; the rest of the words are lower case.

5. Type the words "Master's Abstracts International," a comma, a space, the volume number, and a comma. Underline all of this.

6. Type a space and the page number, followed by a period.

7. Type the University Microfilms reference number in parentheses. Abbreviate the word "Number" as "No."

8. If your reference continues to a second line, doublespace the second line and begin it back at the left margin.

Follow this format exactly.   See Appendix F for a complete list of references.

Jones, J. T. (1993). The effects of bottom-up management techniques on clerical employees in five high-tech companies. Master's Abstracts International, 53, 236. (University Microfilms No. AAD93-12345)

Figure 107. Example of a reference of a Published Thesis Abstracted in MAI and Obtained From University Microfilm.

Referencing a Thesis Abstracted in Master's Abstracts International (MAI) and Obtained From the University

A reference of a published thesis abstracted in MAI and obtained from the University appears in Figure 108 and consists of the following elements:

- Author's name(s)

- Year thesis was copyrighted in DAI

- Title of thesis

- The words "Master's Thesis"

- The name of the university

- The year on the cover page of the disseration

- The words "Master's Abstracts International"

- Volume number

- Page number(s)

To create this reference, follow these steps:

1. Indent one-half inch and type the author's last name in full, followed by a comma and a space.

2. Type the author's first initial (*not* the full first name), a period, a space, the middle initial (if available), then another period and a space. If the author's middle name is not listed, just use the first initial.

Remember: Never, never use the full first name!

3. Type the MAI copyright year in parentheses, followed by a period and a space.

4. Type the thesis title, followed by a period and a space. Only the first word has a capital letter; the rest of the words are lower case.

5. Type an opening parenthesis, then the words "Master's thesis," followed by a comma and a space.

6. Type the name of the university, followed by a comma, a space.

7. Type the year on the cover page of the thesis, followed by the second parenthesis, a space, and a period.

8. Type the words "Master's Abstracts International," a comma, a space, and the volume number. Underline all of this.

9. Type a comma and a space.

10. Type the MAI page number and a period.

11. If your reference continues to a second line, doublespace the second line and begin it back at the left margin.

Follow this format exactly. See Appendix F for a complete list of references.

```
    Jones, J. T. (1993). The effects of bottom-up

management techniques on clerical employees in five

high-tech companies. (Master's thesis, Eastern State

University, 1993). Master's Abstracts International, 53,

642B.
```

Figure 108. Example of a Reference of a Thesis Abstracted in MAI and Obtained From the University.

Referencing an Unpublished Master's Thesis

You might get some material from a thesis on which some-one is currently working. A reference of a unpublished thesis appears in Figure 109 and consists of the following elements:

- Author's name(s)

- Year in which the thesis was written

- Title of thesis

- The words "Unpublished master's thesis"

- The name of the university

- The city (and state, if not in the university name) where the university is located

To create this reference, follow these steps:

1. Indent one-half inch and type the author's last name in full, followed by a comma and a space.

2. Type the author's first initial (*not* the full first name), a period, a space, the middle initial (if available), then another period and a space. If the author's middle name is not listed, just use the first initial.

Remember: Never, never use the full first name!

3. In parentheses, type the year in which the material was written, followed by a period and a space.

4. Type the thesis title, followed by a period, and underline both. Only the first word of the title has a capital letter; the rest of the words are lower case.

5. Type the words "Unpublished master's thesis" in parentheses, followed by a comma and a space.

6. Type the name of the university, followed by a comma and a space.

7. Type the city where the university is located. Follow it with a comma and a space and the two-letter state code if the state is not in the university name.

8. If your reference continues to a second line, doublespace the second line and begin it back at the left margin.

Follow this format exactly. See Appendix F for a complete list of references.

Jones, J. T. (1993). <u>The effects of bottom-up</u>

<u>management techniques on clerical employees in five</u>

<u>high-tech companies.</u> Unpublished master's thesis,

Eastern State University, Elm City, CT.

Figure 109. Example of a Reference of an Unpublished Master's Thesis.

Referencing an Unpublished Manuscript Not Submitted for Publication

You might get some material from a manuscript on which someone is currently working. A reference of a unpublished manuscript not submitted for publication appears in Figure 110 and consists of the following elements:

- Author's name(s)

- Year in which the manuscript was written

- Title of manuscript

- The words "Unpublished manuscript"

To create this reference, follow these steps:

1. Indent one-half inch and type the author's last name in full, followed by a comma and a space.

2. Type the author's first initial (*not* the full first name), a period, a space, the middle initial (if available), then another period and a space. If the author's middle name is not listed, just use the first initial.

Remember: Never, never use the full first name!

3. Type the year in which the material was written in parentheses, followed by a period and a space.

4. Type the manuscript title, followed by a period, and underline both. Only the first word of the title has a capital letter; the rest of the words are lower case.

5. Type the words "Unpublished manuscript" in parentheses, followed by a period.

6. If your reference continues to a second line, doublespace the second line and begin it back at the left margin.

Follow this format exactly. See Appendix F for a complete list of references.

Jones, J. T. (1993). <u>The effects of bottom-up</u> <u>management techniques on clerical employees in five</u> <u>high-tech companies.</u> Unpublished manuscript.

Figure 110. Example of a Reference of an Unpublished Master's Thesis.

Referencing a Manuscript in Progress or Submitted for Publication, But Not Yet Accepted

You might get some material from a manuscript that is in progress or has been submitted for publication, but has not yet been accepted. A reference of a manuscript in progress or submitted for publication, but not yet accepted is shown in Figure 111 and consists of the following elements:

- Author's name(s)

- Year in which the thesis was written

- Title of thesis

- The words "Manuscript in progress" or "Manuscript submitted for publication"

To create this reference, follow these steps:

1. Indent one-half inch and type the author's last name in full, followed by a comma.

2. Type the author's first initial (*not* the full first name), a period, a space, the middle initial (if available), then another period and a space. If the author's middle name is not listed, just use the first initial.

Remember: Never, never use the full first name!

3. Type the year in which the material was written in parentheses, followed by a period and a space.

4. Type the thesis title, followed by a period, and underline both. Only the first word of the title has a capital letter; the rest of the words are lower case.

5. Type the words "Manuscript in progress" or "Manuscript submitted for publication," whichever is applicable. End with a period.

6. If your reference continues to a second line, doublespace the second line and begin it back at the left margin.

Follow this format exactly. See Appendix F for a complete list of references.

Jones, J. T. (1993). <u>The effects of bottom-up</u> <u>management techniques on clerical employees in five</u> <u>high-tech companies.</u> Manuscript submitted for publication.

Figure 111. Example of a Reference of a Manuscript Submitted for Publication, But Not Yet Accepted.

Referencing Unpublished Raw Data From a Study

You might get some material from data someone has collected but has not published. A reference of raw data from a study appears in Figure 112 and consists of the following elements:

- Author's name(s)

- Year in which the material was written

- Title of study

- The words "Unpublished raw data"

To create this reference, follow these steps:

1. Indent one-half inch and type the author's last name in full, followed by a comma and a space.

2. Type the author's first initial (*not* the full first name), a period, a space, the middle initial (if available), then another period and a space. If the author's middle name is not listed, just use the first initial.

Remember: Never, never use the full first name!

3. In parentheses, type the year in which the material was written, followed by a period and a space.

4. Type the topic in brackets to indicate that this is a description of the content, not a title. Only the first word has a capital letter; the rest of the words are lower case..

5. Type a space, then the words "Unpublished raw data," followed by a period.

6. If your reference continues to a second line, doublespace the second line and begin it back at the left margin.

Follow this format exactly. See Appendix F for a complete list of references.

Finlayson, F. D. (1993). [The effects of bottom-up management techniques on clerical employees in five high-tech companies.] Unpublished raw data.

Figure 112. Referencing Unpublished Raw Data From a Study.

Referencing Reviews

This section shows you how to reference a:

- book review

- movie review

- video review

Referencing a Book Review

A reference of a book review appears as shown in Figure 113 and consists of the following elements:

- Author's name(s)

- Year in which the review was copyrighted

- Title of review, if available

- The words "Review of the book"

- Book title

- Name of the magazine or newspaper in which the review appeared

- Volume number, if relevant

- Page number(s)

To create this reference, follow these steps:

1. Indent one-half inch and type the author's last name in full, followed by a comma and a space.

2. Type the author's first initial (*not* the full first name), a period, a space, the middle initial (if available), then another period and a space. If the author's middle name is not listed, just use the first initial.

Remember: Never, never use the full first name!

3. In parentheses, type the year in which the review was written, followed by a period and a space.

4. If the review has a title, continue with this step. If not, go to Step 5.

    Type the title. Only the first word has a capital letter; the rest of the words are lower case.

5. Type the words "Review of the book" and the book title in brackets, followed by a period and a space. Use lower case letters on all words in the title except the first. Underline the book title.

6. Type the name of the magazine or newspaper in which the review appeared and follow it with a comma, a space, the volume number, and a comma. Underline all of these.

7. Type a space, then the page numbers, followed by a period.

8. If your reference continues to a second line, doublespace the second line and begin it back at the left margin.

Follow this format exactly. See Appendix F for a complete list of references.

```
    Jones, J. T. (1993). Exploring new management tech-

niques. [Review of the book The bottom-up approach].

Today's Business, 24, 25-26.
```

Figure 113. Example of a Reference of a Book Review.

Referencing a Movie Review

A reference of a movie review appears as shown in Figure 114 and consists of the following elements:

- Author's name(s)

- Year in which the review was copyrighted

- Title of review, if available

- The words "Review of the film"

- Movie title

- Name of the magazine or newspaper in which the review appeared

- Volume number, if relevant

- Page number(s)

To create this reference, follow these steps:

1. Indent one-half inch and type the author's last name in full, followed by a comma and a space.

2. Type the author's first initial (*not* the full first name), a period, a space, the middle initial (if available), then another period and a space. If the author's middle name is not listed, just use the first initial.

Remember: Never, never use the full first name!

3. Type the year in which the review was written in parentheses, followed by a period and a space.

4. If the review has a title, continue with this step. If not, go to Step 5.

   Type the title. Only the first word has a capital letter; the rest of the words are lower case.

5. In brackets, type the words "Review of the film" and the film title, followed by a period. Underline the film title.

6. Type the name of the magazine or newspaper in which the review appeared, a comma, a space, and the volume number, if relevant, followed by a comma and a space. Underline all of these.

7. Type the page number(s), followed by a period.

8. If your reference continues to a second line, doublespace the second line and begin it back at the left margin.

Follow this format exactly. See Appendix F for a complete list of references.

    Jones, J. T. (1993). Exploring new management tech-
niques [Review of the movie The Bottom-up approach].
Today's Business, 24, 25-26.

Figure 114. Example of a Reference of a Movie Review.

Referencing a Video Review

A reference of a video review appears as shown in Figure 115 and consists of the following elements:

- Author's name(s)

- Year in which the review was copyrighted

- Title of review, if available

- The words "Review of the video"

- Video title

- Name of the magazine or newspaper in which the review appeared

- Volume number, if relevant

- Page number(s)

To create this reference, follow these steps:

1. Indent one-half inch and type the author's last name in full, followed by a comma and a period.

2. Type the author's first initial (*not* the full first name), a period, a space, the middle initial (if available), then another period and a space. If the author's middle name is not listed, just use the first initial.

Remember: Never, never use the full first name!

3. In parentheses, type the year in which the review was written, followed by a period and a space.

4. If the review has a title, continue with this step. If not, go to Step 5.

    Type the title. Only the first word has a capital letter; the rest of the words are lower case. End with a period.

5. In brackets, type the words "Review of the video" and the video title, followed by a period and a space. Underline the video title. Use lower case letters on all words except the first.

6. Type the name of the magazine or newspaper in which the review appeared, a comma, a space, and the volume number, if relevant. Underline all of it.

7. Type a comma and a space, then the page numbers, followed by a period. Do not use the letters "p." and "pp.," since they are not necessary when the reference includes the volume number.

8. If your reference continues to a second line, doublespace the second line and begin it back at the left margin.

Follow this format exactly. See Appendix F for a complete list of references.

```
Jones, J. T. (1993). Exploring new management tech-

niques. [Review of the video The bottom-up approach].

Today's Business, 24, 25-26).
```

Figure 115. Example of a Reference of a Video Review.

Referencing Audio-Visual Materials

This section shows you how to reference a:

- movie

- television broadcast

- television series

- single episode from a television series

- cassette recording

You may find a lot of useful information for your report or project from these sources.

Referencing a Movie

A reference of a movie appears as shown in Figure 116 and consists of the following elements, which you can obtain from the movie's credits:

- Originator's name(s) and title(s)

- Year in which the movie was copyrighted

- Movie title

- The word "Film"

To create this reference, follow these steps:

1. Indent one-half inch and type the originator's last name in full, followed by a comma and a space. The originator can be the executive producer, producer, and/or the director.

2. Type the originator's first initial (*not* the full first name), a period, a space, the middle initial (if available), then a period and a space. If the originator's middle name is not listed, just use the first initial.

Remember: Never, never use the full first name!

3. Type the originator's title in parentheses, followed by a period and a space. (If there are two originators, see the second example in Figure 116.)

4. Type the year in which the movie was copyrighted in parentheses, followed by a period and a space.

5. Type the movie title, underline it, and follow it with a space. Only the first word has a capital letter; the rest of the words are lower case, unless they are proper names.

6. Type the words "Film" in brackets, followed by a period. Be sure to use a capital "F."

7. If your reference continues to a second line, doublespace the second line and begin it back at the left margin.

Follow this format exactly. See Appendix F for a complete list of references.

```
    Smith, R. L. (Producer). (1993). Managing employees
in 90s [Film].
```

```
    Smith, R. L. (Producer), & Jones, L. (Director).
(1993). Managing employees in 90s [Film].
```

Figure 116. Examples of a Reference of a Movie.

Referencing a Television Broadcast

A reference of a television broadcast appears as shown in Figure 117 and consists of the following elements, which you can obtain from the broadcast's credits:

- Originator's name and title

- Year and date of broadcast

- Television broadcast title

- Name of the city from which the broadcast originated

- Production company name

To create this reference, follow these steps:

1. Indent one-half inch and type the originator's last name in full, followed by a comma and a space. The originator can be the executive producer, producer, and/or the director.

2. Type the originator's first initial (*not* the full first name), a period, a space, the middle initial (if available), then a period and a space. If the originator's middle name is not listed, just use the first initial.

Remember: Never, never use the full first name!

3. Type the originator's title in parentheses, followed by a period and a space.

4. In parentheses, type the year in which the show was broadcast, a comma, a space, the month the show was broadcast, the day (do not add "th" or "st"), the second parenthesis, a period, and a space.

5. Type the television show title, a period, and a space. Underline both. Only the first word has a capital letter; the rest of the words are lower case, unless they are proper names.

6. Type the city or cities from which the broadcast originated, followed by a colon and a space.

7. Type the name of the production company, followed by a period.

8. If your reference continues to a second line, doublespace the second line and begin it back at the left margin.

Follow this format exactly. See Appendix F for a complete list of references.

```
    Smith, R. L. (Producer). (1993, August 4). The

business report.  New York: National Broadcasting

Company.
```

Figure 117. Example of a Reference of a Television Broadcast.

Referencing a Television Series

A reference of a television series appears as shown in Figure 118 and consists of the following elements, which you can obtain from the broadcast's credits:

- Originator's name and title

- Year the series aired

- Television series title

- Name of the city from which the series was produced

- Production company name

To create this reference, follow these steps:

1. Indent one-half inch and type the originator's last name in full, followed by a comma and a space. The originator can be the executive producer, producer, and/or the director.

2. Type the originator's first initial (*not* the full first name), a period, a space, the middle initial (if available), then a period and a space. If the originator's middle name is not listed, just use the first initial.

Remember: Never, never use the full first name!

3. Type the originator's title in parentheses, followed by a period.

4. In parentheses, type the year in which the show was broadcast, followed by a period.

5. Type the television show title and a period. Underline both. Only the first word has a capital letter; the rest of the words are lower case, unless they are proper names.

6. Type the city or cities from which the broadcast originated, followed by a colon and a space.

7. Type the name of the production company, followed by a period.

8. If your reference continues to a second line, doublespace the second line and begin it back at the left margin.

Follow this format exactly. See Appendix F for a complete list of references.

```
Smith, R. L. (Producer). (1993). The human experi-

ence. New York: Public Broadcasting Service.
```

Figure 118. Example of a Reference of a Television Series.

Referencing an Episode From a Television Series

A reference of an episode from a television series appears as shown in Figure 119 and consists of the following elements, which you can obtain from the broadcast's credits:

- Scriptwriter's name

- Year the episode aired

- Episode title

- Director's name

- Originator's name

- Series title

- Name of the city from which the series was produced

- Production company name

To create this reference, follow these steps:

1. Indent one-half inch and type the scriptwriter's last name in full, followed by a comma and a space.

2. Type the scriptwriter's first initial (*not* the full first name), a period, a space, the middle initial (if available), then a period and a space. If the scriptwriter's middle name is not listed, just use the first initial.

Remember: Never, never use the full first name!

3. In parentheses, type the year in which the show was broadcast, followed by a period and a space.

4. Type the episode title and underline it. Only the first word has a capital letter; the rest of the words are lower case, unless they are proper names.

5. In parentheses, type the director's first initial and last name, followed by a comma, a space, the word "Director," a period, and a space.

6. Type the word "In," followed by the originator's first initial and last name.

7. In parentheses, type the originator's title. (The originator may be the producer or executive producer.) Type a capital letter on the first word of the title. After the closing parenthesis, type a comma and a space.

8. Type the television series title and a period, and underline both. Only the first word has a capital letter; the rest of the words are lower case, unless they are proper names.

9. Type the city or cities from which the broadcast originated, followed by a colon and a space.

10. Type the name of the production company, followed by a period.

11. If your reference continues to a second line, doublespace the second line and begin it back at the left margin.

Follow this format exactly. See Appendix F for a complete list of references.

Smith, R. L. (1993). <u>The mysterious mind</u> (J. Johnson, Director). In T. Harrison (Executive producer), <u>The human experience.</u> New York: Public Broadcasting Service.

Figure 119. Example of a Reference of an Episode From a Television Series.

Referencing a Cassette Recording

You may listen to a talk on a cassette that you will find useful in your research. A reference of cassette recording appears as shown in Figure 120 and consists of the following elements, which you can obtain from the cassette label or box cover:

- Speaker's name

- The word "Speaker"

- Copyright year

- Cassette title

- Recording number

- Name of the city where the cassette was produced

- Production company name

To create this reference, follow these steps:

1. Indent one-half inch and type the speaker's last name in full, followed by a comma and a space.

2. Type the speaker's first initial (*not* the full first name), a period, a space, the middle initial (if available), then a period and a space. If the speaker's middle name is not listed, just use the first initial.

Remember: Never, never use the full first name!

3. In parentheses, type the word "Speaker," followed by a period and a space.

4. In parentheses, type the copyright year of the cassette, followed by a period and a space.

5. Type the cassette title and underline it. Only the first word has a capital letter; the rest of the words are lower case, unless they are proper names. Type a space.

5. In parentheses, type the cassette recording number, followed by a period and a space. Capitalize the "C," "R," and "N," and abbreviate the word "number" as No."

6. Type the city or cities from which the broadcast originated, followed by a colon and a space.

7. Type the name of the production company, followed by a period.

8. If your reference continues to a second line, doublespace the second line and begin it back at the left margin.

Follow this format exactly. See Appendix F for a complete list of references.

```
    Smith, R. L. (Speaker). (1993). Management Tips

for the 90s (Cassette Recording No. 100-233-66A-B).

New York: Acme Recording Company.
```

Figure 120. Example of a Reference of a Cassette Recording.

Referencing Electronic Media

While there are no real set standards for referencing on-line items yet, the APA has developed some examples based on Li and Crane's (1993) *Electronic Style: A Guide to Citing Electronic Information.* If you are citing an electronic source that is not shown here, please refer to Li and Crane.

This section shows you how to reference a(n):

- on-line abstract

- on-line journal article

- abstract on CD-ROM

- datafile or database

- computer program, software program, or programming language

Referencing an Online Abstract

A reference of an on-line abstract appears as shown in Figure 121 and consists of the following elements:

- Author's name

- Year of publication (if not available, date of search)

- Title of article

- Title of periodical

- The word "on-line"

- The words "Abstract from"

- Path

To create this reference, follow these steps:

1. Indent one-half inch and type the author's last name in full, followed by a comma and a space.

2. Type the author's first initial (*not* the full first name), a period, a space, the middle initial (if available), then a period and a space.

Remember: Never, never use the full first name!

3. In parentheses, type the year of publication (or, if not available, the year of the search), followed by a period and a space.

4. Type the article title, followed by a period and a space. Only the first word has a capital letter; the rest are lower case.

5. In brackets, type "On-line," followed by a period and a space.

6. Type the title of the periodical, a comma, a space, the volume number, and a comma. Underline all of these.

7. Type a space, the page number(s), a period, and a space.

8. Type the words "Abstract from," followed by a colon and a space. Capitalize the "A."

9. Type in the path statement through which this abstract can be located. Do not include a period at the end; doing so may cause retrieval problems for your reader.

10. If your reference continues to a second line, doublespace the second line and begin it back at the left margin.

Follow this format exactly. See Appendix F for a complete list of references.

Johnson, D. W. (1993). Twelve ways to motivate your employees. [On-line]. Management Today, 8, 25-26. Abstract from: DIALOG File: OfficeINFO Item: 20-12345.

Figure 121. Example of a Reference of an On-line Abstract.

Referencing a Subscriber-Based On-line Journal Article

A reference of a subscriber-based on-line journal article appears as shown in Figure 122 and consists of the following elements:

- Author's name

- Date of publication (if not available, date of search)

- Title of article

- Length of article in paragraphs

- Title of periodical

- The words "on-line serial"

- The word "Available"

- Document or accession number

To create this reference, follow these steps:

1. Indent one-half inch and type the author's last name in full, followed by a comma and a space.

2. Type the author's first initial (*not* the full first name), a period, a space, the middle initial (if available), then a period and a space.

Remember: Never, never use the full first name!

3. In parentheses, type the date of publication. Then type a period and a space.

4. Type the article title, followed by a space. Only the first word has a capital letter; the rest are lower case.

5. In brackets, type the length of this article by specifying the number of paragraphs. End with a period and a space.

6. Type the title of the journal and underline it. Type a space.

7. In brackets, type the words "On-line serial." End with a period and a space.

8. Type the word "Available," followed by a colon and a space. Capitalize the "A."

9. Since only subscribers can retrieve this source with the path, type the document or accession number for your reader.

10. If your reference continues to a second line, doublespace the second line and begin it back at the left margin.

Follow this format exactly. See Appendix F for a complete list of references.

```
Johnson, D. W. (1993). Twelve ways to motivate

your employees [25 paragraphs]. Management Today [On-

line serial]. Available: Doc. No. 27
```

Figure 122. Example of a Reference of an Subscriber-Based On-line Journal Article.

Referencing a General-Access On-line Journal Article

You can retrieve general-access on-line journals from two sources:

- E-mail

- FTP

Referencing a General-Access On-line Journal Article from E-mail

A reference of a general-access on-line journal article obtained from E-mail appears as shown in Figure 123 and consists of the following elements:

- Author's name

- Year (and month, if available) of publication

- Title of article

- Length of article in paragraphs

- Title of periodical

- The words "on-line serial"

- Volume and page number

- The words "Available E-mail"

- Path

To create this reference, follow these steps:

1. Indent one-half inch and type the author's last name in full, followed by a comma and a space.

2. Type the author's first initial (*not* the full first name), a period, a space, the middle initial (if available), then a period and a space.

Remember: Never, never use the full first name!

3. In parentheses, type the year (and month, if available) of publication. Follow it with a period and a space.

4. Type the article title. Only the first word has a capital letter; the rest are lower case. Then type a period and a space.

5. In brackets, type the length of this article by specifying the number of paragraphs. End with a period.

6. Type the title of the journal and underline it. Capitalize each word.

7. Type a space. Then, in brackets, type the words "On-line serial." Type another space.

8. Type the volume number, underline it, and place the page number in parentheses. End with a period.

9. Type the words "Available E-mail," followed by a colon and a space.

10. Type the path statement. Do not put any punctuation at the end. It may confuse the reader when retrieving the article.

11. If your reference continues to a second line, doublespace the second line and begin it back at the left margin.

Follow this format exactly. See Appendix F for a complete list of references.

```
Johnson, D. W. (1993, June). Twelve ways to motivate

your employees [25 paragraphs]. Management Today [On-

line serial] 4(14). Available E-mail: psyc@pucc Message:

Get psyc 93-xxxxx
```

Figure 123. Example of a Reference of an General-Access On-line Journal Article Obtained from E-mail.

Referencing a General-Access On-line Journal Article from FTP

A reference of a general-access on-line journal article obtained from FTP appears as shown in Figure 124 and consists of the following elements:

- Author's name

- Year (and month, if available) of publication

- Title of article

- Length of article in paragraphs

- Title of periodical

- The words "on-line serial"

- Volume and page number

- The words "Available FTP"

- Path statement

To create this reference, follow these steps:

1. Indent one-half inch and type the author's last name in full, followed by a comma and a space.

2. Type the author's first initial (*not* the full first name), a period, a space, the middle initial (if available), then a period and a space.

Remember: Never, never use the full first name!

3. In parentheses, type the date, followed by a period and a space.

4. Type the article title, followed by a space. Only the first word has a capital letter; the rest are lower case.

5. In brackets, type the length of this article by specifying the number of paragraphs. End with a period and a space.

6. Type the title of the journal and underline it. Capitalize the first letter of each word in the title.

7. Type a space. Then, in brackets, type the words "On-line serial." Type another space.

8. Type the volume number, underline it, and place the page number in parentheses. End with a period and a space.

9. Type the words "Available FTP," followed by a colon and a space.

9. Type the path statement. Do not end with any punctuation that is not part of the statement. Otherwise, you may confuse the reader during the retrieval process.

10. If your reference continues to a second line, doublespace the second line and begin it back at the left margin.

Follow this format exactly. See Appendix F for a complete list of references.

```
     Johnson, D. W. (1993, June). Twelve ways to motivate

your employees [25 paragraphs]. Management Today [On-

line serial], 4(14). Available FTP: Hostname: princeton.

edu Directory: pub/harnad/Management Today/1993.volume 4

File: management.93.4.14.base-rate.17.funder
```

Figure 124. Example of a Reference of an General-Access On-line Journal Article Obtained From FTP.

Referencing a Datafile or Database

A reference of a datafile or database appears as shown in Figure 125 and consists of the following elements:

- Designer of datafile or database

- Title of datafile or database

- Version number, if applicable

- The words "Electronic datafile" (or "database" or "data tape")

- Year datafile or database was first made available to the public

- Location and name of the producer (person who created the datafile or database)

- The word "Producer"

- Location and name of the distributor (person or company from whom one can order the database or datafile)

- The word "Distributor"

To create this reference, follow these steps:

1. Indent one-half inch and type the primary contributor's name in full, followed by two dashes, then the datafile or database title, followed by a space. The contributor's name is all initial caps; however, only the first word of the title is capitalized.

   Underline the contributor's name and the title.

2. In parentheses, type the version number, followed by a space.

3. In brackets, type the words "Electronic datafile" or "Electronic data tape," or "Electronic database," as applicable. End with a period and a space.

4. In parentheses, type the year this datafile or database was first made available to the public, follwed by a period and a space.

5. Type the city (and state, if needed) where the producer is located, followed by a colon and a space.

6. Type the name of the producer, followed by a space.

7. In brackets, type the word "Producer," followed by a period and a space.

8. Repeat Steps 6 and 7 for the distributor's location and name if different from the producer.

9. If your reference continues to a second line, doublespace the second line and begin it back at the left margin.

Follow this format exactly. See Appendix F for a complete list of references.

American Business Association Survey--Management opportunities in the fortune 500 companies (Version 1) [Electronic datafile]. (1992). Santa Clara, CA: American Business Association [Producer]. San Leandro, CA: Acme Distributors [Distributor].

Figure 125. Example of a Reference of Datafile or Database.

Referencing an Abstract on CD-ROM

A reference of an abstract on CD-ROM appears as shown in Figure 126 and consists of the following elements:

- Author's name

- Year of copyright

- Title of article

- The word "CD-ROM"

- Title of journal

- Volume number, if applicable

- Page numbers

- The words "Abstract from"

- Source and retrieval number

To create this reference, follow these steps:

1. Indent one-half inch and type the author's last name in full, followed by a comma and a space.

2. Type the author's first initial (*not* the full first name), a period, a space, the middle initial (if available), then a period and a space.

Remember: Never, never use the full first name!

3. In parentheses, type the copyright year of this abstract. End with a period and a space.

4. Type the article title. Only the first word has a capital letter; the rest are lower case. End with a period and a space.

5. In brackets, type the word "CD-ROM." End with a period and a space.

6. Type the title of the journal containing this abstract, followed by a comma and a space, then the volume number, followed by a comma. Underline all of these elements.

7. Type the page number(s), followed by a period and a space.

8. Type the words "Abstract from," followed by a colon and a space.

9. Type the source name and retrieval number for this abstract. Do not add punctuation at the end; you may confuse the reader when retrieving the article.

10. If your reference continues to a second line, doublespace the second line and begin it back at the left margin.

Follow this format exactly. See Appendix F for a complete list of references.

```
      Jones, S. L. (1994). Current trends in hepatitis

treatment. [CD-ROM]. Medicine Today, 14, 67-69. Abstract

from: Medical Reports File: MedLIT Item: 20-345
```

Figure 126. Example of a Reference of an Abstract on CD-ROM.

Referencing Computer Materials

You can reference two types of computer materials:

- Software

- Programming languages

A software program or programming language may or may not have an author.

Referencing Computer Software With an Author

A reference of computer software with an author appears as shown in Figure 127 and consists of the following elements:

- Author's name

- Year of copyright

- Title of program

- Version number, if applicable

- The words "Computer program," "Computer software," or "Computer programming language"

- Title of program, software, or programming language

- City where the program, software, or programming language producer is located

- Producer's name

To create this reference, follow these steps:

1. Indent one-half inch and type the author's last name in full, followed by a comma and a space.

2. Type the author's first initial (*not* the full first name), a period, a space, the middle initial (if available), then a period and a space.

Remember: Never, never use the full first name!

3. In parentheses, type the copyright year of this software. End with a period and a space.

4. Type the software title. Only the first word has a capital letter; the rest are lower case. Type a space.

5. In parentheses, type the Version number. Type a space.

6. In brackets, type the word "Computer software," followed by a period and a space.

7. Type the city where the producer is located (and the two-letter state code, if the city is not listed in Table 15), followed by a colon and a space.

8. Type the producer's name. If it is the author(s), type the word "Author" or "Authors" here as shown in Example 2 of Figure 127. End with a period.

9. If your reference continues to a second line, doublespace the second line and begin it back at the left margin.

Follow this format exactly. See Appendix F for a complete list of references.

```
     Rodriguez, J. T. & Vu, P. D. (1993).   The business

report (Version 2.0) [Computer software].   Santa Clara,

CA:  Business News.
```

```
     Rodriguez, J. T. & Vu, P. D. (1993).   The business

report (Version 2.0) [Computer software].   Santa Clara,

CA:  Authors.
```

Figure 127. Examples of a Reference of Computer Software With An Author.

Referencing Computer Software With No Author

A reference of computer software with no author appears as shown in Figure 128 and consists of the following elements:

- Title of program

- The words "Computer software"

- Year of copyright

- City where the program producer is located

- Producer's name

To create this reference, follow these steps:

1. Indent one-half inch and type the program title, followed by a space. Only the first word has a capital letter; the rest are lower case unless they are proper names.

2. In brackets, type the words "Computer software," followed by a period and a space.

3. In parentheses, type the copyright year of this program. End with a period and a space

4. Type the city where the program was produced (and the two-letter state code, if the city is not listed in Table 15 on page 161), followed by a colon and a space.

5. Type the producer's name, followed by a period.

6. If your reference continues to a second line, doublespace the second line and begin it back at the left margin.

Follow this format exactly. See Appendix F for a complete list of references.

```
Buick dimensions 1994 [Computer software]. (1993).

Detroit, MI: General Motors Corporation.
```

Figure 128. Example of a Reference of Computer Software With No Author.

Referencing a Computer Programming Language

A reference of a computer programming language appears as shown in Figure 129 and consists of the following elements:

- Author's name

- Year of copyright

- Title of programming language

- The words "Computer programming language"

- City where the producer is located

- Producer's name

To create this reference, follow these steps:

1. Indent one-half inch and type the author's last name in full, followed by a comma and a space.

2. Type the author's first initial (*not* the full first name), a period, a space, the middle initial (if available), then a period and a space.

Remember: Never, never use the full first name!

3. In parentheses, type the copyright year of this programming language, followed by a period and a space.

4. Type the programming language title. Only the first word has a capital letter; the rest are lower case, unless it is a proper name. Type a space.

5. In brackets, type the words "Computer programming language." Capitalize the "C" on the word "Computer"; the other words are lower case. End with a period and a space.

6. Type the city where the program was produced (and the two-letter state code, if the city is not listed in Table 15), followed by a colon and a space.

7. Type the producer's name, followed by a period. (In the example in Figure 129, the producer is H. V. Chang, so the word "author" is used.)

8. If your reference continues to a second line, doublespace the second line and begin it back at the left margin.

Follow this format exactly. See Appendix F for a complete list of references.

```
Chang, H. V. (1993). V Basic Interpreter [Computer

programming language].  Santa Clara, CA: Author.
```

Figure 129. Example of a Reference of a Computer Programming Language.

Referencing Legal Citations

There are several types of legal references:

- Court cases

- Statutes

- Legislative materials

- Administrative and executive materials

The APA requires that legal citations be referenced with the same information provided in conventional legal formats in legal periodicals. Unlike legal periodicals, however, which list legal citations in footnotes at the bottom of the page, the APA style guide requires legal references to be listed in the References.

For more information on referencing legal materials, please consult *The Bluebook: A Uniform System of Citation* (1991), which the APA follows for legal citation style.

Referencing Court Cases

There are four main types of court cases:

- Court decisions

- Unpublished cases

- Court cases at the trial level

- Court cases at the appellate level

Common abbreviations used in legal references are shown in Table 16. When using these abbreviations, follow the spacing shown exactly.

Table 16. Abbreviations Used in Court References

ABBREVIATION	MEANING
v.	versus
Cong.	U. S. Congress
H.R.	House of Representatives
S.	Senate
Reg.	Regulation
Res.	Resolution
aff'd	affirmed
F.	*Federal Reporter*
F.2d	*Federal Reporter, Second Series*
F. Supp.	*Federal Supplement*
U.S.C.	*United States Code*
Cong. Rec.	*Congressional Record*
Fed. Reg.	*Federal Register*
WL	Westlaw
Jan.	January
Feb.	February
Aug.	August
Sept.	September
Oct.	October
Nov.	November
Dec.	December

Referencing a Court Decision (*Bluebook* Rule 10)

A reference for a court decision appears as shown in Figure 130, and consists of the following elements:

- Name of the decision

- Source volume number

- Source name

- Source page number

- Court name

- Court date

To create this reference, follow these steps:

1. Indent one-half inch and type the name of the decision, followed by a comma and a space. Be sure to use "v." in the decision name.

2. Type the volume number of the published source in which this case is listed, followed by a space.

3a. Type the source name in abbreviated format, followed by a space.

  b. Type the source page number, followed by a space.

4. In parentheses, type the court name. (In Figure 130, "D. Calif." stands for District of California). Then type the date.

5. If your reference continues to a second line, doublespace the second line and begin it back at the left margin.

Follow this format exactly. See Appendix F for a complete list of references.

```
Smith v. Jones, 234 F. Supp. 1394 (D. Calif. 1984).
```

Figure 130. Example of a Reference of a Court Decision.

Referencing an Unpublished Case

There are two types of unpublished cases:

- Filed, but not yet reported

- Unreported decision

Referencing a Case That is Filed, But Not Yet Reported

A reference for a case that is filed, but not yet reported, appears as shown in Figure 131, and consists of the following elements:

- Case name

- Docket number

- Court name in which case was filed

- The word "filed"

- Date of filing

1. Indent one-half inch and type the name of the case, followed by a comma and a space.

2. Type the docket number, followed by a space. Use the Abbreviate "Number" as "No."

3a. In parentheses, type the name of the court in which the case was filed, followed by a space.

   b. Type the word "filed," followed by a space.

   c. Type the date of filing. Abbreviate the month, using the first three letters of its name, then type a period and a space. Type the day, followed by a comma and a space, then the year, followed by the closing parenthesis and a period.

4. If your reference continues to a second line, double-space the second line and begin it back at the left margin.

Follow this format exactly. See Appendix F for a complete list of references.

```
Smith v. Jones, No. 23-1004 (U.S. filed Mar. 3, 1993).
```

Figure 131. Example of a Reference of a Case That is Filed, But Not Reported.

Referencing an Unreported Decision

You can reference an unreported decision from two sources:

- In print

- On LEXIS or Westlaw

REFERENCING AN UNREPORTED DECISION IN PRINT

A reference for an unreported decision in print appears as shown in Figure 132, and consists of the following elements:

- Case name

- Docket number

- The words "slip op."

- Name of the court

- Date of announcement

To create this reference, follow these steps:

1. Indent one-half inch and type the name of the case, followed by a comma, and a space.

2. Type the docket number. Abbreviate "Number" as "No." End with a comma, and a space.

3. Type the words "slip op.," followed by a space. ("Slip op." is short for "slip opinion"—an opinion not published in a case reporter, but printed separately, due to its recency.)

4a. In parentheses, type the name of the court in which the case was filed, followed by a space.

  b. Type the word "filed," followed by a space.

  c. Type the date of filing. Begin by abbreviating the name of the month and following it with a period and a space. Type the date, followed by a comma, then the year, followed by the closing parenthesis and a period.

5. If your reference continues to a second line, double-space the second line and begin it back at the left margin.

Follow this format exactly. See Appendix F for a complete list of references.

```
     Smith v. Jones, No. 23-1004 (U.S. filed Mar. 3, 1993).
```

```
     Smith v. Jones, No. 23-1004, slip op. at [10]. (U.S.

filed Mar. 3, 1993).
```

Figure 132. Example of a Reference of an Unreported Decision in Print.

REFERENCING AN UNREPORTED DECISION ON LEXIS OR WESTLAW

You can find unreported cases on LEXIS or Westlaw, too. These electronic databases are a tremendous resource for finding legal materials. A reference of an unreported decision found here may or may not have a record number.

Referencing an Unreported Decision on LEXIS or Westlaw With a Record Number

A reference with a record number appears as shown in Figure 133, and consists of the following elements:

- Case name

- Docket number

- Decision year

- Court name

- LEXIS or Westlaw record number

- Screen page number

- District name

- Date of decision

To create this reference, follow these steps:

1. Indent one-half inch and type the name of the case, followed by a comma, and a space.

2. Type the docket number, a comma, and a space. Abbreviate "Number" as "No."

3. Type the decision year and court name.

4. Type the LEXIS or Westlaw record number, a comma, and a space.

5. Type the word "at," a space, an asterisk, and the screen page number. (The asterisk is used to distinguish this page number from a slip op page number.)

6a. In parentheses, type the name of the court in which the case was filed.

 b. Type the date of filing. Abbreviate the month, if necessary. Follow it with a period and a space. Type the date, a comma, a space, the year, the closing parenthesis, and a period.

7. If your reference continues to a second line, doublespace the second line and begin it back at the left margin.

Follow this format exactly. See Appendix F for a complete list of references.

```
    Gomez v. Sanders Corp., No. 45-1234, 1993 U.S. Dist.

WL 19284, at *4 (D. Kan. Dec. 13, 1993).
```

Figure 133. Example of a Reference of an Unpublished Case Found on Westlaw With a Record Number.

Referencing an Unreported Decision on LEXIS or Westlaw Without a Record Number

A reference without a record number appears as shown in Figure 134, and consists of the following elements:

- Case name

- Docket number

- Court name

- Date of decision

- Source name and other identifying information

To create this reference, follow these steps:

1. Indent one-half inch and type the name of the case, followed by a comma, and a space.

2. Type the docket number and a space.

3a. In parentheses, type the name of the court in which the case was filed, followed by a period and a space.

  b. Type the date of filing. Abbreviate the month, if necessary. Follow it with a period and a space. Type the day, a comma, a space, the year, the closing parenthesis, and a space.

4. In parentheses, type the database name and any other identifying information.

5. If your reference continues to a second line, double-space the second line and begin it back at the left margin.

Follow this format exactly. See Appendix F for a complete list of references.

```
Williams v. ABC Manufacturing, No.12-4567 (D. Calif.

Feb. 25, 1994) (LEXIS, Genfed library, Dist file).
```

Figure 134. Example of a Reference of an Unpublished Case Found on LEXIS With No Record Number.

Referencing a Court Case at the Trial Level

You can reference trials at two levels:

- State trial court

- Federal district court

Referencing a State Trial Court Case

A reference of a state trial court case appears as shown in Figure 135, and consists of the following elements:

- Case name

- Source volume number

- Source name

- Source page number

- Court name

- Year of decision

To create this reference, follow these steps:

1. Indent one-half inch and type the name of the case, followed by a comma and a space.

2a. Type the source volume number and a space.

b. Type the source name and a space.

c. Type the source page number and a space.

3. In parentheses, type the court name and decision date, followed by a period.

4. If your reference continues to a second line, double-space the second line and begin it back at the left margin.

Follow this format exactly. See Appendix F for a complete list of references.

```
        Williams v. ABC Manufacturing, 14 Pa. D. & C.4th 136
(C.P. Washington County 1991).
```

Figure 135. Example of a Reference of a State Trial Court Case.

Referencing a Federal District Court Case

A reference of a federal district court case appears as shown in Figure 136, and consists of the following elements:

- Case name

- Source volume number

- Source name

- Source page number

- Court name

- Year of decision

To create this reference, follow these steps:

1. Indent one-half inch and type the name of the case, followed by a comma and a space.

2a. Type the source volume number and a space.

  b. Type the source name and a space.

  c. Type the source page number and a space.

3. In parentheses, type the court name and decision date, followed by a period.

4. If your reference continues to a second line, double-space the second line and begin it back at the left margin.

Follow this format exactly. See Appendix F for a complete list of references.

```
        Williams v. ABC Manufacturing, 456 F. Supp. 234
(D. Calif. 1989).
```

Figure 136. Example of a Reference of a Federal District Court Case.

Referencing a Court Case at the Appellate Level

Court cases can be appealed to one of two courts:

- State supreme court

- State court of appeals

Referencing a Court Case Appealed to a State Supreme Court

A reference of a court case appealed to a state supreme court appears as shown in Figure 137, and consists of the following elements:

- Case name

- Source volume number

- Source name

- Source page number

- Year of decision

To create this reference, follow these steps:

1. Indent one-half inch and type the name of the case, followed by a comma, and a space.

2a. Type the source volume number and a space.

  b. Type the source name and a space.

  c. Type the source page number and a space.

3. In parentheses, type the decision date, followed by a period.

4. If your reference continues to a second line, double-space the second line and begin it back at the left margin.

Follow this format exactly. See Appendix F for a complete list of references.

```
Williams v. ABC Manufacturing, 456 Calif. 234 (1989).
```

Figure 137. Example of a Reference of a Court Case Appealed to a State Supreme Court.

Referencing a Court Case Appealed to a State Court of Appeals

A reference of a court case appealed to a state court of appeals appears as shown in Figure 138, and consists of the following elements:

- Case name

- Source volume number

- Source name

- Source page number

- Court name

- Year of decision

To create this reference, follow these steps:

1. Indent one-half inch and type the name of the case, followed by a comma, and a space.

2a. Type the source volume number and a space.

b. Type the source name and a space.

c. Type the source page number and a space.

3. In parentheses, type the court name and decision date, followed by a period.

4. If your reference continues to a second line, double-space the second line and begin it back at the left margin.

Follow this format exactly. See Appendix F for a complete list of references.

```
    Williams v. ABC Manufacturing, 234 S.W.2d 234 (Calif.

Ct. App. 1989).
```

*Figure 138. Example of a Reference of a Court Case Appealed to a State
          Court of Appeals.*

Referencing Statutes

You can reference statutes from two sources:

- State code

- Federal code

Referencing a Statute in a State Code

A reference for a statute in a state code appears as shown in Figure 139 and consists of the following elements:

- Name of act

- Volume number

- Source

- Section number

- Any other references to the act

To create this reference, follow these steps:

1. Indent one-half inch and type the name of the act, followed by a comma and a space.

2. Type the volume number, followed by a space.

3. Type the source name, followed by a space.

4. Type the section symbol(s), followed by a space, and the section number(s), followed by a comma.

5. In parentheses, type any other references to the act, followed by a period.

6. If your reference continues to a second line, doublespace the second line and begin it back at the left margin.

Follow this format exactly. See Appendix F for a complete list of references.

```
        Mental Care and Treatment Act, 4 Kan. Stat. Ann.

§§ 59-2901-2941 (1983 & Supp. 1992).
```

Figure 139. Example of a Reference of a Statute in a State Code.

Referencing a Statute in a Federal Code

A reference for a statute in a federal code appears as shown in Figure 140 and consists of the following elements:

- Name of act and year passed

- Volume number

- Source

- Section number

- Publisher of volume, if relevant

- Year volume was published

To create this reference, follow these steps:

1. Indent one-half inch and type the name of the act, followed by a comma and a space.

2. Type the volume number, followed by a space.

3. Type the source name, followed by a space.

4. Type the section symbol, followed by a space, and the section number.

5. In parentheses, type the name of the publisher, if relevant, a space, and the year the volume was published, followed by a period.

6. If your reference continues to a second line, doublespace the second line and begin it back at the left margin.

Follow this format exactly. See Appendix F for a complete list of references.

```
     National Environmental Policy Act of 1969,

44 U.S.C.A. § 4332 (West 1976).
```

Figure 140. Example of a Reference of a Statute in a Federal Code.

Referencing Legislative Materials (Bluebook Rule 13)

Legislative materials include:

- testimony at hearings

- full hearings

- unenacted federal bills and resolutions

- enacted bills and resolutions

- federal reports and documents

Referencing Testimony at a Hearing

A reference for testimony at a hearing appears as shown in Figure 141 and consists of the following elements:

- Title of hearing as stated on official pamphlet

- Congressional number

- Session number

- Page number of pamphlet

- Year testimony was given

- The words "testimony of" and the testifier's name

To create this reference, follow these steps:

1. Indent one-half inch and type the hearing title, followed by a period and a space. Include the bill number, if relevant; the submittee name, if relevant; and the committee name. Underline this entire entry.

2. Type the Congressional number, followed by a comma and a space.

3. Type the session number, followed by a space.

4. Type the page number in the pamphlet where the testimony is documented.

5. In parentheses, type the year in which the testimony was given.

6. In parentheses, type the name of the person whose testimony you are referencing. End with a period.

7. If your reference continues to a second line, doublespace the second line and begin it back at the left margin.

Follow this format exactly. See Appendix F for a complete list of references.

<u>RU486: The Import Ban and Its Effect on Medical Research: Hearings Before the Subcommittee on Regulation, Business Opportunities, and Energy, of the House Committee on Small Business</u>. 101st Cong., 2d Sess. 35 (1990) (testimony of Ronald Chesemore).

Figure 141. Example of a Reference of Testimony at a Hearing.

Referencing a Full Hearing

A reference for a full hearing appears as shown in Figure 142 and consists of the following elements:

- Title of hearing as stated on official pamphlet

- Congressional number

- Session number

- Page number of pamphlet

- Year testimony was given

To create this reference, follow these steps:

1. Indent one-half inch and type the hearing name, followed by a period and a space. Include the bill number, if relevant; the submittee name, if relevant; and the committee name. Underline this entire entry.

2. Type the Congressional number, followed by a comma and a space.

3. Type the session number, followed by a space.

4. Type the page number in the pamphlet where the testimony is documented.

5. In parentheses, type the year in which the testimony was given. End with a period.

6. If your reference continues to a second line, double-space the second line and begin it back at the left margin.

Follow this format exactly. See Appendix F for a complete list of references.

RU486: The Import Ban and Its Effect on Medical

Research: Hearings Before the Subcommittee on Regula-

tion, Business Opportunities, and Energy, of the House

Committee on Small Business. 101st Cong., 2d Sess. 35

(1990).

Figure 142. Example of a Reference of a Full Hearing.

Referencing an Unenacted Federal Bill or Resolution

A reference for an unenacted federal bill or resolution appears as shown in Figure 143 and consists of the following elements:

- Title, if available

- Source name

- Bill or resolution number

- Congressional or Senate number

- Session number

- The abbreviation "Sess."

- Section number, if relevant

- Year bill or resolution was introduced

To create this reference, follow these steps:

1. Indent one-half inch and type the bill or resolution name, followed by a comma and a space.

2. Type the source name (H.R. for House of Representatives or S. for Senate), a space, and the bill or resolution number, followed by a comma and a space.

3. Type the Senate or Congressional number (use just "d" for "second" or "third"), followed by a comma and a space.

4. Type "Sen" for "Senate," or "Cong" for Congress, followed by a period and a space.

5. Type the session number (use just "d" for "second" or "third"), followed by a space and the abbreviation "Sess." for "session."

6. In parentheses, type the section symbol, a space, and the section number.

6.   In parentheses, type the year in which the bill or
       resolution was introduced.

7.   If your reference continues to a second line, double-
       space the second line and begin it back at the left
       margin.

Follow this format exactly. See Appendix F for a complete
list of references.

```
    Space Memorial Bill,  S. 5936,  102d Cong.,  2d Sess.

§ 4 (1992).
```

*Figure 143. Example of a Reference of an Unenacted Federal Bill or
       Resolution.*

Referencing an Enacted Federal Bill or Resolution

A reference for an enacted federal bill or resolution appears as shown in Figure 144 and consists of the following elements:

- Source and title, if available

- Bill or resolution number

- Congressional or Senate number

- The abbreviation "Cong." or "Sen."

- Session number

- The abbreviation "Sess." for "Session"

- Volume number

- Source

- Page number

- Year bill or resolution was passed

To create this reference, follow these steps:

1. Indent one-half inch and type the source name ("H.R. Res." for House of Representatives Resolution or "S. Res." for Senate Resolution) and the bill or resolution number, followed by a comma and a space.

2. Type the Congressional or Senate number, followed by a comma and a space.

3. Type the abbreviation "Cong" or "Sen," followed by a period and a space.

4. Type the session number, followed by a space.

5. Type the abbreviation "Sess," followed by a period and a space.

6. Type the source volume number, followed by a space.

7. Type the source name in abbreviated form, followed by a space.

8. Type the page number, followed by a space.

9. In parentheses, type the year in which the bill or resolution was passed.

10. If your reference continues to a second line, doublespace the second line and begin it back at the left margin.

Follow this format exactly. See Appendix F for a complete list of references.

```
    S. Res. 107, 103d Cong., 1st Sess. 139 Cong. Rec.
107, 5826 (1993).
```

Figure 144. Example of a Reference of an Enacted Federal Bill or Resolution.

Referencing a Federal Report or Document

A reference for a federal report or document appears as shown in Figure 145 and consists of the following elements:

- Report or document number

- Congressional number

- Session number

- Year report or document was published

To create this reference, follow these steps:

1. Indent one-half inch and type the source name ("H.R. Rep." or "H.R. Doc." for House of Representatives Report or Document, or "S. Rep." for Senate Report or Document) and the report or document number, followed by a comma and a space.

2. Type the Congressional number, followed by a comma and a space.

3. Type the session number, followed by a space.

4. Type the year in which the report or document was published.

5. If your reference continues to a second line, doublespace the second line and begin it back at the left margin.

Follow this format exactly. See Appendix F for a complete list of references.

S. Rep. No. 234, 103d Cong., 1st Sess. (1993).

or

S. Doc. No. 234, 103d Cong., 1st Sess. (1993).

Figure 145. Examples of a Reference of a Federal Report or Document.

Referencing Administrative and Executive Materials

You can reference two types of administrative and executive materials:

- Federal rules and regulations
- Executive orders

Referencing a Federal Rule or Regulation

A reference for a federal rule or regulation appears as shown in Figure 146 and consists of the following elements:

- Title of the rule or regulation
- Number of the rule or regulation
- Volume number
- Source
- Section number
- Year in which the rule or regulation was passed

To create this reference, follow these steps:

1. Indent one-half inch and type the rule or regulation title (and number, if relevant), a comma and a space.

2. Type the volume number, followed by a space.

3. Type the section symbol, followed by a space.

4. Type the section number, followed by a space.

5. Type the year the rule or regulation was passed.

6. If your reference continues to a second line, doublespace the second line and begin it back at the left margin.

Follow this format exactly. See Appendix F for a complete list of references.

```
FTC Credit Practices Rule, 16 C.F.R. § 444 (1991).
```

Figure 146. Example of a Reference of a Federal Regulation.

Referencing an Executive Order

A reference for an executive order appears as shown in Figure 147 and consists of the following elements:

- Executive order number

- Volume number of the Code of Federal Regulations

- Page number

- Year in which the executive order was passed

To create this reference, follow these steps:

1. Indent one-half inch and type the executive order number, a comma, and a space. Abbreviate as "Exec. Order No."

2. Type the volume number, followed by a space.

3. Type the abbreviation C.F.R., followed by a space.

4. Type the page number, followed by a space.

5. Type the year the executive order was issued, followed by a period.

6. If your reference continues to a second line, doublespace the second line and begin it back at the left margin.

Follow this format exactly. See Appendix F for a complete list of references.

```
Exec. Order No. 12804, 3 C.F.R. 298 (1992).
```

Figure 147. Example of a Reference of an Executive Order.

Alphabetizing References

To alphabetize references, follow the rules in Table 17.

Table 17. Rules for Alphabetizing References in the Reference List.

RULE	EXAMPLES
1. List names in alphabetical order by last name of the first author	Gold, T. M. Golding, S. A.
2. Alphabetize the prefixes M', Mc, and Mac literally	MacIntyre McGill M'Connell
3. Alphabetize last names containing articles and prepositions by the rules of the language of origin. Refer to the biographical section of *Webster's Collegiate Dictionary* for detailed help.	Aldenbruck, B. von D'Angelo, T. L. de la Salandra, M. G. De Santos, C. R. DuBois, J. J. Van Handel, S. L. Von Richtofen, P. D.
4. Alphabetize references beginning with numbers as if the numbers were spelled out.	5 Rules for Good Management. (1994). Forbes, M. T. (1993).
5. Alphabetize multiple works by the same author(s) by year of publication, the earliest first.	Garrison, J. T. (1989). Garrison, J. T. (1994). Jansen, L. M. & Chung, H. L. (1991). Jansen, L. M. & Chung, H. L. (1993).
6. Alphabetize one-author works before multiple author works with that same author.	Garrison, J. T. (1994) Garrison, J. T. & Taylor, B. R. (1992).
7. Alphabetize works with the same first author and different second or third authors by the name of the second (then third) author.	Garrison, J. T. & Marcos, L. N. (1993). Garrison, J. T. & Taylor, B. R. (1992). Garrison, J. T. & Taylor, B. R. & Javier, S. A. (1993).
8. Alphabetize works by the same author(s) with the same publication date by the title (do not count "A" or "The") and place "a," "b," etc., after the publication date.	Campbell, M. R. (1992a). The ethics of management. Campbell, M. R. (1992b). The theory of TQM.
9. Alphabetize works by different first authors with the same last name by the first initial. Include the author's initials in the text citation.	Lewis, B. T. (1993). Lewis, S. D. (1991).
10. Alphabetize works with group authors or no authors by the first significant word of the name or of the title, if no name is listed. Treat legal references likewise. If the work is listed as Anonymous, place this word, spelled completely out, as the author, and listed alphabetically in the "A" listings.	

Chapter 8

Punctuation and Spelling

The APA uses punctuation rules derived from *Words into Type* (Skillin and Gay, in press) and the *Chicago Manual of Style* (University of Chicago, 1993). For information on punctuation not shown in in this chapter, please consult these books.

This chapter explains the APA requirements of:

- commas, quotation marks, brackets, and slashes

- spelling

- numbering volumes in the reference list

Punctuation Requirements and Exceptions

Table 18 shows the punctuation requirements; Table 19 shows the exceptions to those requirements.

Table 18. APA Punctuation Requirements

PUNCTUATION	WHERE USED	EXAMPLE
Comma	Between elements in a series of three or more items	. . .two managers, three employees, and five clients.
Double quotation marks	To introduce a word or phrase used as an ironic comment, slang, or as an invented or coined expression.	
	To set off the title of an article or chapter in a magazine or book when mentioned in the text.	Smith's (1992) article, "The Paperless Office," focuses on the use of . . . .
Brackets	To enclose parenthetical material within parentheses; use commas, if possible.	

Table 19. Punctuation Exceptions

PUNCTUATION	DO NOT USE	TYPE AS
Comma	to separate parts of measurement	6 years 4 months
Slash	in these phrases: and/or pretest/posttest	Monday, Tuesday, or both pretest and posttest

Spelling Requirements

Table 20 shows the spelling requirements of the APA style for creating plurals of the words shown.

Table 20. Spelling Requirements

SINGULAR	PLURAL	SINGULAR	PLURAL
appendix	appendixes	matrix	matrices
datum	data	phenomenon	phenomena

Numbering Requirements

Table 21 shows the numbering requirements when listing a volume in the references. Note that you must use an Arabic numeral, not a Roman numeral.

Table 21. Numbering Requirements

EXAMPLE	APA STYLE REQUIREMENT
Vol. IV	Vol. 4

Bibliography

The following books were used as source material for The World's Easiest Guide to Using the APA:

American Psychological Association
      1994 *Publication Manual of the American Psychological Association.* Fourth Edition. Washington, DC: Author.

Harvard Law Review Association
      1991 *The Bluebook: A Uniform System of Citation* (15th ed.). Cambridge, MA: Author.

Appendix A

Sample Report With
One Heading Level

NOTE: *The example presented in this appendix is meant for viewing of heading levels only. The length of each section as shown here is not an indication of the length that your sections should be; these sections are abbreviated due to space limitations.*

Marketing Strategies to Increase Revenue

in Acme Widgets' Western Region

Lorem ipsum dolor sit amet, consectetuer adipiscing elit, sed diam nonummy nibh euismod tin cidunt ut laoreet dolore magna aliquam erat volutpat. Ut wisi enim ad minim veniam, quis nostrud exerci tation ullamcorper suscipit lobortis nisl ut aliquip ex ea commodo consequat.

Findings

Lorem ipsum dolor sit amet, consectetuer adipiscing elit, sed diam nonummy nibh euismod tin cidunt ut laoreet dolore magna aliquam erat volutpat. Ut wisi enim ad minim veniam, quis nostrud exerci tation ullamcorper suscipit lobortis nisl ut aliquip ex ea commodo consequat.

Duis atem vel eum iriure dolor in hendrerit in vulputate velit esse molestie consequat, vel illum dolore eu feugiat nulla facilisis at vero eros et accumsan et iusto odio dignissim qui blandit praesent luptatum zzril delenit augue duis dolore te feugait nulla facilisi.

Conclusion and Recommendations

Duis atem vel eum iriure dolor in hendrerit in vulputate velit esse molestie consequat, vel illum dolore eu feugiat nulla facilisis at vero eros et accumsan et iusto odio dignissim qui blandit praesent luptatum zzril delenit augue duis dolore te. nostrud exerci tation ullamcorper suscipit lobortis nisl ut facilisis at vero eros et accumsan et iusto odio dignissim qui blandit praesent luptatum zzril delenit augue duis dolore te aliquip ex ea commodo consequat.

Appendix B

Sample Report With Two Heading Levels

NOTE: *The example presented in this appendix is meant for viewing of heading levels only. The length of each section as shown here is not an indication of the length that your sections should be; these sections are abbreviated due to space limitations.*

Marketing Strategies to Increase Revenue

in Acme Widgets' Western Region

Lorem ipsum dolor sit amet, consectetuer adipiscing elit, sed diam nonummy nibh euismod tin cidunt ut laoreet dolore magna aliquam erat volutpat. Ut wisi enim ad minim veniam, quis nostrud exerci tation ullamcorper suscipit lobortis nisl ut aliquip ex ea commodo consequat.

Vel Illum Dolore

Lorem ipsum dolor sit amet, consectetuer adipiscing elit, sed diam nonummy nibh euismod tin cidunt ut laoreet dolore magna aliquam erat volutpat. Ut wisi enim ad minim veniam, quis nostrud exerci tation ullamcorper suscipit lobortis nisl ut aliquip ex ea commodo consequat.

Duis atem vel eum iriure dolor in hendrerit in vulputate velit esse molestie consequat, vel illum dolore eu feugiat nulla facilisis at vero eros et accumsan et iusto odio dignissim qui blandit praesent luptatum zzril delenit augue duis dolore te feugait nulla facilisi.

Feugiat Nulla Facilisis at Vero Eros et Accumsan et Iusto Odio Dignissim Qui Blandit

Lorem ipsum dolor sit amet, consectetuer adipiscing elit, sed diam nonummy nibh euismod tin cidunt ut laoreet dolore magna aliquam erat volutpat. Ut wisi enim ad minim veniam, quis nostrud exerci tation ullamcorper suscipit lobortis nisl ut velit esse molestie consequat, vel illum dolore eu feugiat nulla aliquip ex ea commodo consequat. Odio dignissim qui blandit praesent luptatum zzril delenit.

Nostrud Exerci Tation Ullamcorper

Lorem ipsum dolor sit amet, consectetuer adipiscing elit, sed diam nonummy nibh euismod tin cidunt ut laoreet dolore magna aliquam erat volutpat. Ut wisi enim ad minim veniam, quis nostrud exerci tation ullamcorper suscipit lobortis nisl ut aliquip ex ea commodo consequat.

Nonummy Nibh Euismod

Duis atem vel eum iriure dolor in hendrerit in vulputate velit esse molestie consequat, vel illum dolore eu feugiat nulla facilisis at vero eros et accumsan et iusto odio dignissim qui blandit praesent luptatum zzril delenit augue duis dolore te feugait nulla facilisi. Nam liber tempor cum soluta nobis eleifend option congue nihil imperdiet doming id quod mazim placerat facer possim assum:

Conclusions and Recommendations

Ut wisi enim ad minim veniam, quis nostrud exerci tation ullamcorper suscipit lobortis nisl ut aliquip ex ea commodo consequat. Duis atem vel eum iriure dolor in hendrerit in vulputate velit esse molestie consequat, vel illum dolore eu feugiat nulla facilisis at vero eros et accumsan et iusto odio dignissim qui blandit praesent.

Appendix C

Sample Chapter/Report With Three Heading Levels

NOTE: *The example presented in this appendix is meant for viewing of heading levels only. The length of each section as shown here is not an indication of the length that your sections should be; these sections are abbreviated due to space limitations.*

Chapter One

Introduction

The Research Problem

Problem statement/purpose. Lorem ipsum dolor sit amet, consectetuer adipiscing elit, sed diam nonummy nibh euismod tin cidunt ut laoreet dolore magna aliquam erat volutpat.

Background of the problem. Lorem ipsum dolor sit amet, consect etuer adipiscing elit, sed diam nonummy nibh euismod tin cidunt ut laoreet dolore magna aliquam erat volutpat. Ut wisi enim ad minim veniam.

Basic research questions. Duis atem vel eum iriure dolor in hendrerit in vulputate velit esse molestie consequat, vel illum dolore eu feugiat nulla facilisis at vero eros et accumsan et iusto odio dignissim qui blandit praesent luptatum zzril delenit augue duis dolore te sed diam nonummy nibh euismod tin cidunt ut laoreet dolore magna aliquam erat volutpat. Ut wisi enim ad minim veniam. Duis etem feugait nulla facilisi:

1. Nam liber tempor cum soluta nobis eleifend option congue nihil?
2. Imperdiet doming id quod mazim placerat facer possim assum?

Ut wisi enim ad minim veniam, quis nostrud exerci tation ullamcorper suscipit lobortis nisl ut aliquip ex ea commodo consequat.

Operational Definitions

Dependent and independent variables. Nam liber tempor cum soluta nobis eleifend option. Ut wisi enim ad minim veniam, quis nostrud exerci tation ullamcorper suscipit. Duis atem vel eum iriure dolor in hendrerit in vulputate velit esse molestie consequat, vel illum dolore eu feugiat nulla facilisis at.

Technical and other terms. Duis atem vel eum iriure dolor in hendrerit in vulputate velit esse molestie consequat, vel illum dolore eu feugiat nulla facilisis at vero eros et accumsan et iusto odio dignissim qui blandit praesent luptatum zzril delenit augue duis dolore te feugait nulla facilisi.

Hypotheses and Sample

Hypotheses. Duis atem vel eum iriure dolor in hendrerit in vulputate velit esse molestie consequat:

H_0. Lorem ipsum dolor sit not amet, consectetuer adipiscing.

H_1. Lorem ipsum dolor sit amet, consectetuer adipiscing.

H_0. Ut wisi not enim ad minim veniam, quis nostrud exer tation.

H_2. Ut wisi enim ad minim veniam, quis nostrud exerci.

Scope. Nam liber tempor cum soluta nobis eleifend option congue nihil imperdiet doming id quod mazim placerat facer possim assum.

Limitations. Lorem ipsum dolor sit amet, consectetuer adipiscing. Facilisis et iusto odio dignissim euismod. Ut wisi enim ad minim veniam, quis nostrud exerci tation ullamcorper suscipit lobortis nisl ut aliquip ex ea commodo consequat.

General Procedures

Duis atem vel eum iriure dolor in hendrerit in vulputate velit esse molestie consequat, vel illum dolore eu feugiat nulla facilisis at vero eros et accumsan et iusto odio dignissim qui blandit praesent luptatum zzril delenit.

Summary

Duis atem vel eum iriure dolor in hendrerit in vulputate velit esse molestie consequat, vel illum dolore eu feugiat nulla facilisis at vero eros et accumsan et iusto odio dignissim qui blandit praesent luptatum zzril delenit augue duis dolore te feugait nulla facilisi.

Appendix D

Sample Chapter/Report With Four Heading Levels

NOTE: *The example presented in this appendix is meant for viewing of heading levels only. The length of each section as shown here is not an indication of the length that your sections should be; these sections are abbreviated due to space limitations.*

Chapter One

Introduction

The Research Problem

Problem Statement/Purpose

Lorem ipsum dolor sit amet, consectetuer adipiscing elit, sed diam nonummy nibh euismod tin cidunt ut laoreet dolore magna aliquam erat volutpat. Ut wisi enim ad minim veniam, quis nostrud exerci tation ullamcorper suscipit lobortis nisl ut aliquip ex ea commodo consequat.

Background of the Problem

Lorem ipsum dolor sit amet, consectetuer adipiscing elit, sed diam nonummy nibh euismod tin cidunt ut laoreet dolore magna aliquam erat volutpat. Sed diam nonummy nibh euismod tin cidunt ut laoreet dolore magna aliquam erat volutpat. Ut wisi enim ad minim veniam, quis nostrud exerci tation ullamcorper suscipit lobortis nisl ut aliquip ex ea commodo consequat.

Basic Research Questions

Duis atem vel eum iriure dolor in hendrerit in vulputate velit esse molestie consequat:

1. Nam liber tempor cum soluta nobis eleifend option congue nihil?
2. Imperdiet doming id quod mazim placerat facer possim assum?
3. Ut wisi enim ad minim veniam, quis nostrud exerci tation?
4. Ullamcorper suscipit lobortis nisl ut aliquip ex ea commodo consequat?

<u>Operational Definitions</u>

<u>Dependent and Independent Variables</u>

<u>Dependent variables.</u> Nam liber tempor cum soluta nobis eleifend option congue nihil imperdiet doming id quod mazim placerat facer possim assum. Ut wisi enim ad minim veniam, quis nostrud exerci tation.

<u>Independent variables.</u> Lorem ipsum dolor sit amet, consectetuer adipiscing elit, sed diam nonummy nibh euismod tin cidunt ut laoreet dolore magna aliquam erat volutpat. Ut wisi enim ad minim veniam, quis nostrud exerci tation ullamcorper suscipit lobortis nisl ut aliquip ex.

<u>Technical and Other Terms</u>

Nam liber tempor cum soluta nobis eleifend option congue nihil imperdiet doming id quod mazim placerat facer possim assum:

LOREM   Quis nostrud exerci tation ullamcorper.

IPSUM   Consectetuer adipiscing elit, sed diam nonummy
          nibh euismod.

<u>Hypotheses and Sample</u>

<u>Hypotheses</u>

Duis atem vel eum iriure dolor in hendrerit in vulputate velit esse molestie consequat:

H_0. Lorem ipsum not dolor sit amet, consectetuer adipiscing elit.

H_1. Lorem ipsum dolor sit amet, consectetuer adipiscing elit.

H_0. Ut wisi not enim ad minim veniam, quis nostrud exerci tation
       ullamcorper not suscipit.

H_2. Ut wisi enim ad minim veniam, quis nostrud exerci tation
       ullamcorper suscipit.

Scope

    Nam liber tempor cum soluta nobis eleifend option congue nihil imperdiet doming id quod mazim placerat facer possim assum. Lorem ipsum dolor sit amet, consectetuer adipiscing elit, sed diam nonummy nibh euismod tin cidunt ut laoreet dolore magna aliquam erat volutpat. Nam liber tempor cum soluta nobis eleifend option congue nihil imperdiet doming id quod mazim placerat facer possim assum.

General Procedures

    Duis atem vel eum iriure dolor in hendrerit in vulputate velit esse molestie consequat, vel illum dolore eu feugiat nulla facilisis at vero eros et accumsan et iusto odio dignissim qui blandit praesent luptatum zzril delenit augue duis dolore te feugait nulla facilisi. Lorem ipsum dolor sit amet, consectetuer adipiscing elit, sed diam nonummy nibh euismod tin cidunt ut laoreet dolore magna aliquam erat volutpat. Nam liber tempor cum soluta nobis eleifend option congue nihil imperdiet doming id quod mazim placerat facer possim assum.

    Lorem ipsum dolor sit amet, consectetuer adipiscing elit, sed diam nonummy nibh euismod tin cidunt ut laoreet dolore magna aliquam erat volutpat. Ut wisi enim ad minim veniam, quis nostrud exerci tation ullamcorper suscipit lobortis nisl ut aliquip ex. Nam liber tempor cum soluta nobis eleifend option congue nihil imperdiet doming id quod mazim placerat facer possim assum. Ut wisi enim ad minim veniam, quis nostrud exerci tation.

Summary

Duis atem vel eum iriure dolor in hendrerit in vulputate velit esse molestie consequat, vel illum dolore eu feugiat nulla facilisis at vero eros et accumsan et iusto odio dignissim qui blandit praesent luptatum zzril delenit augue duis dolore te feugait nulla facilisi. Ut wisi enim ad minim veniam, quis nostrud exerci tation ullamcorper suscipit lobortis nisl ut aliquip ex. Nam liber tempor cum soluta nobis eleifend option congue nihil imperdiet doming id quod mazim placerat facer possim assum. Ut wisi enim ad minim veniam, quis nostrud exerci tation.

Appendix E

Sample Chapter/Report With Five Heading Levels

NOTE: *The example presented in this appendix is meant for viewing of heading levels only. The length of each section as shown here is not an indication of the length that your sections should be; these sections are abbreviated due to space limitations.*

CHAPTER FOUR

RESULTS AND FINDINGS

Lorem ipsum dolor sit amet, consectetuer adipiscing elit, sed diam nonummy nibh euismod tin cidunt ut laoreet dolore magna aliquam erat volutpat. Ut wisi enim ad minim veniam, quis nostrud exerci tation ullamcorper suscipit lobortis nisl ut aliquip ex ea commodo consequat.

Results and Findings

Lorem ipsum dolor sit amet, consectetuer adipiscing elit, sed diam nonummy nibh euismod tin cidunt ut laoreet dolore magna aliquam erat volutpat. Ut wisi enim ad minim veniam, quis nostrud exerci tation ullamcorper suscipit lobortis nisl ut aliquip ex ea commodo consequat. Sed diam nonummy nibh euismod tin cidunt ut laoreet dolore. Aliquam erat volutpat. Ut wisi enim ad minim veniam, quis nostrud exerci tation ullamcorper suscipit lobortis nisl ut aliquip ex ea commodo consequat.

ABC Company

Management Response

First group. Lorem ipsum dolor sit amet, consectetuer adipiscing elit, sed diam nonummy nibh euismod tin cidunt ut laoreet dolore magna aliquam erat volutpat. Sed diam nonummy nibh euismod tin cidunt ut laoreet dolore.

Second group. Duis atem vel eum iriure dolor in hendrerit in vulputate velit esse molestie consequat, vel illum dolore eu feugiat nulla facilisis at vero eros et accumsan et iusto odio dignissim.

Employee Response

First group. Lorem ipsum dolor sit amet, consectetuer adipiscing elit, sed diam nonummy nibh euismod tin cidunt ut laoreet dolore magna aliquam erat volutpat. Ut wisi enim ad minim veniam, quis nostrud exerci tation ullamcorper suscipit lobortis nisl ut aliquip ex ea commodo consequat.

Second group. Nam liber tempor cum soluta nobis eleifend option congue nihil imperdiet doming id quod mazim placerat facer possim assum. Lorem ipsum dolor sit amet, consectetuer adipiscing elit.

XYZ Company

Management Response

First group. Lorem ipsum dolor sit amet, consectetuer adipiscing elit, sed diam nonummy nibh euismod tin cidunt ut laoreet dolore magna aliquam erat volutpat. Ut wisi enim ad minim veniam, quis nostrud exerci tation ullamcorper suscipit lobortis nisl ut aliquip ex ea commodo consequat.

Second group. Duis atem vel eum iriure dolor in hendrerit in vulputate velit esse molestie consequat, vel illum dolore eu feugiat nulla facilisis at vero eros et accumsan et iusto odio dignissim qui blandit praesent luptatum zzril delenit augue duis dolorre te feugait nulla facilisi.

Employee Response

First group. Lorem ipsum dolor sit amet, consectetuer adipiscing elit, sed diam nonummy nibh euismod tin cidunt ut laoreet dolore magna aliquam erat volutpat. Ut wisi enim ad minim veniam, vel illum dolore eu feugiat nulla facilisis at vero

eros et accumsan et iusto odio. Quis nostrud exerci tation ullamcorper suscipit lobortis nisl ut aliquip ex ea commodo consequat.

Second group. Nam liber tempor cum soluta nobis eleifend option congue nihil imperdiet doming id quod mazim placerat facer possim assum. Lorem ipsum dolor sit amet, consectetuer, adipiscing elit, sed diam nonummy nibh euismod tin cidunt ut laoreet dolore magna aliquam erat volutpat.

Analysis

Duis atem vel eum iriure dolor in hendrerit in vulputate velit esse molestie consequat, vel illum dolore eu feugiat nulla facilisis at vero eros et accumsan et iusto odio dignissim qui blandit praesent luptatum zzril delenit augue duis dolore te feugait nulla facilisi. Nam liber tempor cum soluta nobis eleifend option congue nihil imperdiet doming id quod mazim placerat facer possim assum.

Lorem ipsum dolor sit amet, consectetuer adipiscing elit, sed diam nonummy nibh euismod tin cidunt ut laoreet dolore magna aliquam erat volutpat. Ut wisi enim ad minim veniam, quis nostrud exerci tation ullamcorper suscipit lobortis nisl ut aliquip ex ea commodo consequat. Sed diam nonummy nibh euismod tin cidunt ut laoreet dolore. Aliquam erat volutpat. Ut wisi enim ad minim veniam, quis nostrud exerci tation ullamcorper suscipit lobortis nisl ut aliquip ex ea commodo consequat.

Summary

Nam liber tempor cum soluta nobis eleifend option congue nihil imperdiet doming id quod mazim placerat facer possim assum. Lorem ipsum dolor sit amet, consectetuer adipiscing elit, sed diam nonummy nibh euismod tin cidunt ut laoreet dolore magna aliquam erat volutpat. Lorem ipsum dolor sit amet, consectetuer adipiscing elit, sed diam nonummy nibh euismod tin cidunt ut laoreet dolore magna aliquam erat volutpat. Ut wisi enim ad minim veniam, quis nostrud exerci tation ullamcorper suscipit lobortis nisl ut aliquip ex ea commodo consequat.

Appendix F

Sample List of References

REFERENCES

American Management Association (1992). PCs today. New York: Author.

Harrison, P. R. (1989). The manager's world (F. G. Taylor, Ed.). Los Angeles: Business Press.

Jones, J. (Ed.). (1992). PCs today. New York: Acme Press.

Kendall, J. T. (1992). The workplace in the year 2000. In 21st century business. New York: Doubleday.

Lopez, T. L. (1992). The workplace in the year 2000. In J. Jones (Ed.), PCs today (pp. 201-210). New York: Acme Press.

Morrison, H. A. (1992, December). The paperless office. Business Talk, 115, 70-76.

Parris, C. A. (1969). Mastering executive arts and skills. New York: Atheneum.

RU486: The Import Ban and Its Effect on Medical Research: Hearings Before the Subcommittee on Regulation, Business Opportunities, and Energy, of the House Committee on Small Business. 101st Cong., 2d Sess. 35 (1990) (testimony of Ronald Chesemore).

S. 5936, 102d Cong., 2d Sess. § 4(1992).

Spetch, M. L., & Wilkie, D. M. (1983). How to bullet-proof your manuscript. New York: Atheneum.

The student's dictionary (4th Ed.). (1992). New York: Wallace Company.

Index

About the Author

Carol J. Amato is a writer, editor, anthropologist, and educator. As a writer, she has published ten books, over 75 articles, and two short stories. She has written software user manuals, training guides, policy and procedure manuals, marketing materials, and general business documents for software development firms, banks, aerospace, and commercial industry.

Her editorial experience includes eleven books, two book series, and numerous articles, and has served as editor for two magazines. She is a guest lecturer, has given many papers at conferences, and has appeared on television and radio shows.

As an anthropologist, she has conducted research in the social and psychological problems associated with living in isolated and confined environments, such as undersea labs, Arctic and Antarctic research labs, space habitats, submarines, oil tankers, etc.

An adjunct faculty member of the University of Phoenix (San Diego and Southern California campuses) and Golden West College, Ms. Amato teaches business and technical writing classes. She served as the Area Chair of Communications at the UOP San Diego campus from 1990-1994. In addition, she has taught at the junior high and high school levels, both in the United States and in England.

Ms. Amato has a B.A. in Spanish and French from the University of Portland in Portland, Oregon, and an M.A. in Environmental Anthropology from California State University, Fullerton, California. She is a board member of International PEN, Orange County Chapter; the Writer's Club of Whittier, Inc., a professional writers' workshop; and the current president of the Professional Writers of Orange County. She was a board member of the Orange County Section of the Independent Writers of Southern California from 1988-1993. She is listed in Who's Who of American Women, Who's Who in the West, Who's Who in Orange County, and the World Who's Who of Women.

STARGAZER
Publishing Company

PO Box 2178
Westminster, CA 92683
(800) 606-7895
(714) 531-6342
FAX (714) 531-8898

READER COMMENT CARD

We have tried to make these instructions accurate, complete, and readable, yet understandable to the undergraduate. Please take a moment to tell us what you think.

How useful was *The World's Easiest Guide to Using the APA* in completing your report, project, or thesis?

❑ Excellent   ❑ Good   ❑ Average   ❑ Poor

Check what you feel are the best features of this reference guide:

_____ well-organized   _____ clearly written   _____ well-illustrated   _____ fully-researched

Should anything be added?

_____

_____

_____

_____

Should anything be deleted or corrected?   Please give the page, paragraph, and line number, and a brief explanation here:

_____

_____

_____

_____

_____

What is your overall rating of this reference guide?

❑ Excellent   ❑ Good   ❑ Average   ❑ Poor

Your name _____

College name _____Phone_____

Address _____

City _____ State _____ ZIP _____

Thank you for your time!

STARGAZER

Publishing Company
PO Box 2178
Westminster, CA 92683

STARGAZER
Publishing Company
PO Box 2178
Westminster, CA 92683
(800) 606-7895
(714) 531-6342
FAX (714) 531-8898

ORDER FORM

 **Yes!** Rush me *The World's Easiest Guide to Using the APA.* 368 pages, softcover, 8½" x 11".

QUANTITY	ISBN	DESCRIPTION	LIST PRICE	AMOUNT
_____	0-9643853-4-1	College Edition, Spiral Bound	$19.95	$_____
_____	0-9643853-5-X	Library Edition, Perfect Bound	$19.95	$_____
		Sales tax 7.75% (CA residents only)		$_____
		SUBTOTAL		$_____
		Shipping/handling for individual orders only: $2.75 per book 4th class, $4.50 per book First Class		$_____
		TOTAL		$_____

Method of Payment: ❏ Check ❏ Money Order ❏ VISA ❏ Mastercard ❏ Amex ❏ Discover

Card Number_____

Expiration Date _____Signature_____

INSTITUTIONAL ORDERS

Resale number: _____ P. O. Number:_____

Shipping Method: ❏ UPS Ground   ❏ Next-day Air   ❏ 2nd Day Air   ❏ Library Rate

SHIP TO:

Name _____

Institution _____

Address _____

City_____State_____Zip_____

All orders must be prepaid unless accompanied by an institutional purchase order number.
UPS cannot deliver to PO boxes.

"The World's Easiest Style Guides"

Publishing Company
PO Box 2178
Westminster, CA 92683